CLIMB YOUR EVEREST

*A Journey of Adventure, Adversity, and Absolution
Inspired by the Women, Life, Freedom Movement in Iran*

Sara Safari PhD

Dedication

This book is dedicated to the courageous and resilient girls and women supported by the Climb Your Everest Non-Profit Organization.

I also dedicate this book to my parents, in their selflessness, I have found inspiration to push my limits and embrace challenges. Their constant presence has instilled in me the values of dedication, perseverance, and resilience, which have been the driving forces behind the creation of this work.

Mom and Dad, your belief in my abilities has been the wind beneath my wings, propelling me forward even in the face of adversity. As I dedicate this book to you, I hope to honor your unwavering support and acknowledge that every achievement is a reflection of the foundation you have laid for me.

Acknowledgements

My heartfelt gratitude extends to my vast network of friends and family who've graciously endured my extended absences during my overseas endeavors and mountain-climbing expeditions in distant lands.

Special recognition goes to Climb Your Everest board members for their invaluable support and dedication in providing insights, leadership, and a strong commitment to furthering our cause.

My deepest appreciation is reserved for my countless Nepali friends and volunteers who have selflessly lent their support to this cause. Their involvement has been instrumental in creating opportunities for young girls and women who otherwise may have been denied access to education.

I extend a heartfelt thank you to my dear guides and friends Garret Madison, Vern Tejas, Terray Sylvester, Robert Smith, Reagan, Amin Kh, Funuru & Luke who captured these unforgettable moments and shared these incredible journeys with me in Nepal. Your companionship and support have made these experiences truly remarkable.

Dr. Sara Safari

Table of Contents

Preface

You might have watched my survival and rescue from the 2015 earthquake depicted in the Netflix documentary "Aftershock". This book starts with the devastating 7.8 earthquake that shook my life; however, this book is my journey as the first Iranian woman to climb the highest peaks on each of the seven continents (known as the Seven Summits). I climbed all these mountains to raise funds and awareness for 7 different nonprofit organizations that are empowering women globally. I am sharing everything that I have learned during my 10 year journey to complete this quest.

Within these pages, you will not only find tales of adventure and valor but also a poignant illustration of how the altruistic efforts of a select few can bring hope and transformation to countless others who have faced abandonment, neglect, or abuse. It underscores the immense power of leading by example, of making a difference through our daily actions, rather than merely relying on monetary contributions or prescriptive directives. Our successes in aiding and rescuing hundreds of girls were not solely a product of financial support and educational programs, but rather the deep connections we formed through mentoring and fostering relationships, inviting them to tread the path we've forged.

Every single penny of the profit from this book goes directly to support the Climb Your Everest, a registered 501(c)(3) nonprofit organization. Your contributions are not only impactful but also fully tax deductible.

"Climb Your Everest" captures the essence of our daily struggles and aspirations. Each of us faces our own unique challenges, aspirations, and goals that parallel the monumental feat of conquering the Mount Everest. This book invites you to embark on a transformative journey where you'll explore the parallels between scaling the world's highest peak and overcoming the obstacles that shape our lives.

Within these pages, you'll find narratives of personal triumph, resilience, and growth as we navigate the complexities of work, education, relationships, health, and personal well-being. Just as climbers ascend the daunting slopes of Everest, we too ascend the peaks of our own lives, determined to reach new heights.

Before delving into the practical guidance provided in the workbook at the end of Chapter 15, immerse yourself in the stories and insights shared throughout the book. Engage with the experiences of those who have faced challenges head-on, confronting their fears and embracing their aspirations. Allow these narratives to resonate with your own journey and inspire you to view your daily struggles as opportunities for growth and empowerment.

As you read "Climb Your Everest," you'll discover that the summit isn't just a destination; it's a mindset. It's about embracing the journey, no matter how steep the incline or treacherous the terrain. The stories within these pages remind us that while the path to success may be challenging, the rewards are immeasurable.

Once you've absorbed the wisdom and insights offered in the book, turn to the accompanying workbook. Here, you'll find thought-provoking questions, reflective exercises, and practical strategies designed to guide you on your own ascent toward personal and professional fulfillment. By engaging with the workbook, you'll delve deeper into your aspirations, confront your fears, and harness the power of your own determination to reach your Everest.

Chapter 1

The Biggest Earthquake in My Life

On April 25, 2015. I had just conquered the toughest stretch of the route, maneuvering around deep crevasses and scaling the final wall to reach Camp 1 at 20,000 feet. It was snowing, freezing cold even though it was almost noon. My legs were tired, but my spirit was still up as I approached the top of that last ladder. Each step felt difficult, but I was focused on timing my exhales with each rung I touched. I knew I was just an hour or two away from the goal.

Taking a breather, I gazed around, soaking in the surreal landscape and pondering how I had landed myself here. It was like an ice wonderland, with these massive caves, towering blocks of frozen ice, and cracks that seemed to plummet into an abyss. For two years, I had been practicing for this moment, arranging ladders on chairs in my room, practicing my steps with spiked crampons tied tight to my heavy-duty mountain boots. Yet, let me confess, every second spent in this danger zone, I was a bundle of nerves, constantly checking the clock for safety's arrival.

The past month had been all about climbing up thousands of feet, coming back down for a breather, letting our bodies adjust. And now, we were ascending into what they call the 'death zone.' Jets fly here, and your body instantly begins to fall apart. Lungs fill with fluid, brains scream for an escape. Over 200 bodies are frozen in the mountain's icy embrace, like eerie sculptures. Those who fell in the icefall are now swallowed by the glacier, and they'll eventually find their way back to Base Camp in a couple of centuries.

Our mission for this trip was to reach Camp 2 and return, followed by another round of training before our final push for the summit. The journey had been incredibly smooth so far. Well, except for the numbing cold. Oh, and the ladders. And of course, the unpredictable twists of the icefall.

I found myself clinging to this ladder, the fifth one stacked high against a sheer wall in the Khumbu Icefall, the castle gate guarding the entrance to the Everest. This place is wild and unpredictable. Imagine, it's where 16 Sherpa guides lost their lives in a tragic accident the year before, and it's where many climbers trying to reach the summit never make it. The ground opens up beneath you without a warning. Towers of ice suddenly collapse, sending ice chunks the size of cars tumbling down. This glacier, almost like a living creature, grows and changes the whole landscape, keeping you on your toes.

I must have crossed more ladders than I could even keep track of, definitely over 50! They were everywhere, some leaning precariously over deep icy gaps called crevasses, others set against walls. Those vertical ones were my jam because if I tripped, there was a fighting chance of survival, being securely anchored. But there was this rumor going around that if you lost your footing on those tightrope-like walks over the grand canyons of ice, you'd plummet all the way back to the good ol' USA. So, I chanted in my head, 'Don't look down, just step easy and chill.' The sound of my crampons scraping the metal rungs was annoying me, and my entire focus was on where I put each foot; one wrong move and I'd probably take down the climbers behind me like dominoes.

Our climbing group set out from Base Camp around 5 AM, which felt like a late morning brunch by Everest standards. Most of the other squads had set off ages before us, smartly dodging the risks of melting ice and potential avalanches as the sun got cozy with the glacier. Our crew was a mix of six climbers and two guides, and guess where I was? Right in the middle, just where I like it.

"Holler when it's clear!" I yelled, my voice coming out like a rough whisper that barely sounded like me, as I hit the top of a ladder. That was my cue for the folks behind me to follow suit, so I hoofed it up the next ladder to reach a ledge where we could take a breather.

This year, the route through the icy maze was entirely new. They shook things up after the tragic chaos of the previous year when an avalanche turned Everest into a deadly playground. Those brave Sherpas were setting ropes and doing the most important job, when things went south, ensuring that summiting was just not in the cards for anyone. So here we were, following this fresh pathway that zigzagged through and around obstacles like an extreme version of hopscotch. And you know what? Things were looking darn good: our team was a united force with no weak links, everyone had each other's back. The weather prediction? A total win. Despite our lazy start, we were trucking along, making solid headway toward camp and the finish line was just a hop, skip, and a jump away.

Those ladders? Man, even when they were bolted tight into the ice, they still had this constant jiggling and shifting going on. Sometimes they decided to scoot a little from the weight of us climbers going up and over. The ice itself was a mover and a shaker, letting out groans that could almost pass for human.

I was just about to grab on the next ladder rung and hoist myself up when things took a dreadful turn. The ladder was solid on the wall, but the whole deal started swaying left and right like a tipsy dancer. Suddenly, it felt like I was falling – but gripping tighter didn't seem to be helping much. It was like the entire mountain was going rogue. Which, in a way, it was.

In an instant, I was in a snow globe gone haywire. Snow was everywhere, and a mean wind was trying to give me wings (not the good kind). My brain couldn't quite process the pandemonium, and I was left wondering why everything decided to go kablooey. Best I could think of was, 'Grab that rope above the ladders and haul your butt to safety.' Down below, someone was shouting, 'Avalanche!' but, hello, I'm a Southern Californian – my brain knows an earthquake when it feels one. This quake would clock in at 7.8, taking over 10,000 lives, including almost 20 climbers and staff back at Base Camp.

Slow steps? Nah, that was history. Now, I was climbing faster than a squirrel in caffeine mode, yanking on that rope above me like it owed me money. I sneak a glance over my shoulder – ice towers are dropping like confetti. The spot we took a breather at? Kapoof! Vanished. If we'd lounged for a few more minutes, we'd have been inside a snow hurricane smoothie.

Ice chunks are breaking off left and right, and visibility? Ha, what's that? Now, I'm getting the full avalanche experience, a mix of debris and blowing snow that's got me all kinds of disoriented. All I can think about is up, up, up – until I finally drag myself over the wall on my stomach. I'm hyperventilating like I just ran a marathon on Mars, gasping for air like my lungs are on fire. I try to buckle up to as many anchors as I can find, though I know that's like building a sandcastle against a tidal wave. Wind's so nuts I'm surprised it didn't give me flight, so I'm hugging the ground like a rodeo rider on a bucking bronco.

I wrap a rope around my hand and arm, tying it to an anchor like it's my lifeline. Can't feel my fingers, I'm so cold. My face? It's like someone dropped an ice cube tray on it. My heart is pounding like it's auditioning for a heavy metal band. I keep telling myself, 'Hold on, keep breathing,' as if my life depends on it. Which, turns out, it did.

The avalanche is bearing down, wind whipping like crazy. I've got that rope in a death grip, and I'm using my crampons to nail myself to the ice for dear life. There's a moment – brief, but forever – where everything just pauses. And in that heartbeat, I know. I'm thinking, 'This is how it ends.' I'm feeling an odd peace, accepting that I might be done for. I hold on like a rodeo cowboy, waiting for whatever the mountain decides.

Above the roaring winds, a guide's voice floats – asking if I'm good. Others are screaming out their locations. But I'm like a human maraca, my legs have gone all salsa dancer on me. I can't move, can't control myself. My hands are squeezing that rope for dear life, going tense and then slack like a rubber band. I try to catch a deep breath, but it's more like a sob. Over the next hours, our team somehow finds each other, all alive, and I can't stop the tears. The radio's buzzing with news that folks down at Base Camp are crushed, boulders and ice playing bowling with them. And those higher up? Stuck at Camp 2, no way to come down.

Then, a head pops up over the wall. It's Kate, my tent buddy. We've been through thick and thin, and I'd bet Everest on her making it. She's got this mix of determination and desperation on her face, holding up her hand – 'Can't feel my fingers. Can't feel my fingers.' I start crawling her way, then the mountain throws another curveball and I hold on like it's a life raft.

Seeing my friend, reality slaps me harder. This mom of four might lose her fingers. And that shakes me up even worse than being buried. I start hyperventilating again, can't catch my breath. I flip onto my back, surrounded by snow swirls. We're trapped up here, no way down. Ladders? Poof, gone

After we regrouped at the top of the wall, we kind of huddled together, clutching each other like we'd just survived a wild rollercoaster. News was buzzing in from radios and satellite phones, painting a grim picture of the chaos unfurling across Nepal. Over 100,000 kids were suddenly homeless, heaps of people buried under rubble in Kathmandu, and entire villages erased in the Annapurna Himalayas to our west. I figured that by now, folks back home probably thought I was an ice popsicle – the mountain had shut down all summit attempts, and it looked like a repeat of last year's summit shutdown.

Honestly, I was ready to plop down in the snow, catch my breath, and let it all sink in. But those guides? They were all about pushing us uphill, like a bunch of determined drill sergeants. Problem was, the trail was gone – the avalanche had turned it into a snow smoothie. There were more ladders ahead, but they looked sketchy, barely hanging onto the ice. And our minds were on everyone else – those below, those above – how could anyone have pulled through that madness?

When we finally hit camp, my eyes zoomed in on this guide from another team, standing in front of his tent, eyes welled up like a waterfall. News had just hit him about the disaster at Base Camp. But my thoughts? I started thinking about the girls who I just raised money for them to continue their education. They were miles away! Are they ok? My mission was to plant the flag of Empower Nepali Girls (ENG) up there on the summit. These past years, we've been backing up mostly lower caste girls who are like prime targets for human trafficking and early marriage. ENG provided scholarships and mentorship for them, keeping them in school and out of harm's reach. Over 300 girls were part of the program, many of them the first-ever higher education trailblazers in their villages. Our first cohort was on the path to becoming doctors, nurses, teachers, and engineers. They'd never seen women with careers like mine – a professor, an engineer, a woman who had braved the male-dominated world of the Middle East. They were blown away that I could out-muscle most guys, climb higher and farther than the lot. It fired them up. It planted hope. It was like a sneak peek into what life could hold for them. But then this earthquake swooped in and kicked our dreams in the gut. Their homes, schools – poof, vanished.

I'd sworn to raise a dollar for each foot of Everest (all 29,028 of 'em) to help these girls, and guess what? I smashed that goal like a champ even though it was my first time fundraising for anything. But now, it felt like everything I'd worked for had been sucked into a black hole. My eyes, man, they were leaking like faucets, and no matter how many folks tried to offer comfort, I was like a lost cause. I'd put so much muscle into spotlighting these kids' struggles in Nepal, and now a lot of those stars-in-the-making could be swallowed by this earthquake chaos. So much lost, so much dashed, so much pain. I couldn't stop crying!

I was very traumatized! Julie, a doctor from a different team, took a glance at me and her face went, 'Oh no.' My brain was doing the cha-cha, totally scrambled from the ordeal. I'd lost all bearings – who, what, where, you name it. I was this disoriented shivering mess, half from sheer terror and half from the freeze digging into my bones. Julie did not mess around. She grabbed me, yelled into the wind, 'Sara! Inside. Now. Seriously, you're gonna end up a human popsicle!' She practically dragged me into a tent and then, get this, she starts playing clothes-chef, peeling off my wet gear –

boots, crampons, Jackets, hat. Sounds simple, but my gear was frozen like Elsa's favorite braids. I'm still shivering, shaking, crying rivers, and the last thing I hear before blacking out is Julie's voice, all reassuring, 'Hey, don't worry, it's all good.'

I woke up from that hazy nap who-knows-when, to a chorus of frantic chit-chat outside. People were piecing together a puzzle of disaster – who's gone, what's wrecked. Once I managed to glue my brain back together and slip into something cozy, I ventured outside. Turns out, we were now mountain hostages with a limited buffet of supplies. That fancy icefall we came through? One-way ticket. Helicopter rescue? Good luck with that, folks said. The altitude and this wild weather weren't exactly helicopter fan-faves. And if we did somehow pull a Houdini and make it back to Base Camp, the trail home was vaporized, like a trail of breadcrumbs gobbled up by a hungry trail monster.

Back in the tent I crawled, passed out again, and got the wakeup call of the year: another earthquake and an avalanche serenade from Nuptse, Everest's neighbor sister. Cue the guide yelling – 'Tents shut, helmets on, or you'll be hang-gliding without the glider!'

I was stuck in that tent for two nights, waiting for a superhero rescue. I mean, I was dead tired and cold as an ice cube most of the time. All I did was burrow deeper into my sleeping bag, fully dressed and all. Oh, and I kept that waterworks show going – couldn't shut off the faucet. The earth decided to have a fit, sending aftershocks our way like unwanted party crashers. Each time those tremors hit, we'd clutch tighter to our sanity, thinking the ground might just swallow us up before the chopper could even get here.

My mind was doing these somersaults about my family, my mom, my dad – they must be a wreck, wondering if I was alive, well, or buried in snow somewhere. But the girls – our girls – that was a whole another level of worry. If they lost homes, or worse, their lives, I couldn't even imagine.

And then, like an answer to frozen prayers, one morning I kinda woke up (or did I?), and there it was – this muffled hum, like a dying bumblebee trying to land. A helicopter. I swear, the thin air and the crazy winds were making this pilot throw chairs and whatever out the door, like a Marie Kondo session, high-altitude style. We were ordered to leave our gear, only women could take the first flight. And let me tell ya, in that moment, being a woman was like winning the lottery. It was the first time in my life that I was happy I am a woman.

We flew down to the Base Camp in a few minutes, chopper racing back to scoop up the left-behinds. Just a few days ago, this place was like a rowdy carnival. Laughter, music, summit tales – the whole deal. Now? Ghostville, but with a side of haunting. Clothes splattered with blood, tents turned into pancake piles, gear strewn like a kid's toys on the lawn. It was like the aftermath of a rock 'n' roll party that went way off the rails. People, survivors, they were walking around, eyes blank, looking for their buddies who were now just mountain memories. It was unbelievable. It was one of the saddest days of my life. I think I will process that day for the rest of my life.

Fast forward – five more days of camping out in this tragic theme park. We could not hike down the mountain due to dangerous route and landslides so we eventually helicoptered down. Finally, the last chopper showed up and we were airlifted to Lukla Airport. I had these big plans, you know? Walking down from the summit successfully, playing tag with the girls, swapping stories, sharing snacks, giving a hand with homework. But now I was worried that if I could ever see them again. I'd gathered up extra food from fellow climbers, all set to play snack fairy. No one will use these snacks since we will go back home soon so I better distribute them between my girls. But reality was a hard slap. I jumped off that chopper and raced to where their homes used to be. Manila, one of our rockstar girls, spotted me and we did this silent nod – like, "Yep, we're in this together." She took me on this grim tour, showing me the damage, checking on kids, and doing what little we could to add a spark of help in a really dark time. We found most of the girls and they were not injured physically but very traumatized.

"Hey, please, come back for us," those girls would tell me on repeat, like a broken record. It's a line I've heard time and again because loads of folks who hit Nepal for treks and climbs drop promises like confetti and then vanish into thin air. ENG, though? ENG has been active in this country for 15 solid years, so we've earned some credibility around these parts especially in women empowerment work. But those girls, they've seen their fair share of empty vows from many others, so they're skeptical. They're worried that we're just another "gone with the wind" story.

So, what did I do? I pinky swore, virtually speaking, over and over. "I'm coming back, guys. Seriously. You're stuck with me. We're in this together. Homes, schools, lives – we're fixing it all, like a human toolkit. I promise you."

Finally after days, back in Kathmandu, after a bumpy ride from the mountains, I got smacked with the big picture. Turns out, the quake's slap wasn't reserved just for Everest. The capital city, this ancient wonderland of monasteries and temples, was now a crumpled mess. Imagine a giant hand shuffling your favorite board game – that's what happened here. The ground decided to throw a tectonic tantrum, lifting the city up and shoving it south, wrecking those old brick-and-mud beauties. And you know who was in the eye of this devastation storm? Yep, those scholarship girls – the ones who were putting their all into shaping a future, only to have the floor disappear from under them.

Chapter 2

Empower Nepali Girls

Returning home felt surreal. My mind kept drifting back to the modest home of one of the girls I visited during my last trip. A tiny room made of stone and mud, barely spacious enough for one person, yet her entire family somehow shared that space. Now, even that humble abode was wiped away.

At the airport, my family welcomed me with flowers and signs, relief etched across their faces. As they hugged me, their worried glances focused on my fingers, ensuring they were all intact. I didn't know how to express what I felt. Looking at my mom, I could see the toll my journey had taken on her. Guilt weighed heavily on me – I had caused so much concern and yet, here I was, safe and sound at home, not with the girls who needed me so desperately.

Before we even settled into the car, the question that loomed was whether I planned to return to Nepal. I gazed out the window, lost in thought, and their frustration was palpable. "That's absurd! You can't go back there after what happened! That mountain nearly took your life."

Speechless, I felt a numbness, an emptiness. It was as if a part of me had been left behind on Everest, and I wasn't sure if I'd ever recover it. I had intended to leave mementos for our scholarship girls near the summit – letters, notes, little stuffed animals – all lost in the avalanche, scattered across the Himalayas. Just looking at my duffel bags filled with climbing gear, the items I managed to retrieve, brought back memories I desperately wanted to forget. I sat there, tears streaming down my face, a scene that had become all too familiar since my return.

A call from my aunt in Iran, checking on my well-being, resonated deeply. She implored me never to return to Nepal, urging me to start a family as a good Iranian wife should. At 34, with no children in sight, I felt the weight of societal expectations. "Sara," she chided, "you're approaching 40. It's time to settle down."

Her words invoked comparisons with my mother, who had four kids by 27. I tried to explain, "I'm not ready yet. There are things I need to do first." Uncertain of what those things were, I grappled with my promise to start a family after conquering Everest. While I doubted I'd return to the mountain anytime soon, a return to Nepal was an urgent need.

Everyone around me worried! I was different now, changed in some unexplainable way. Nightmares jolted me awake! Perhaps I needed to take care of myself, to rediscover what I had lost. I remembered the silent meditation retreat before a training climb – it had been a challenge in its own right. Maybe I needed to embark on a similar journey now.

The earthquake didn't just shake the ground; it shook my marriage too. I sensed a growing distance between my husband and me, a gap that had been carved out by the countless hours I dedicated to mountain training. The thought lingered: Had my pursuit of climbing mountains damaged our relationship? I aimed to inspire Nepali girls to chase their dreams, and I had to lead by example. But now, I grappled with doubt: What if this was all a terrible mistake?

Overwhelmed by guilt, shame, and a sense of failure, I felt far from empowered. The girls' faces haunted me; I was meant to uplift them, yet I had become a burden. While I enjoyed creature comforts at home, I couldn't forget the children living with so little. I wished I could go back to Nepal, helping those in need while I grappled with my own emotions.

"Despite everything, you did empower those girls," a friend reassured me, sensing my depression. "You raised an incredible amount of money for them, more than you ever imagined. And an earthquake of that magnitude could have stopped anyone from reaching the summit. Those girls must be proud of you."

The words were comforting, but it was hard to shake off the weight of suffering I had witnessed. My friends, however, pledged to support my mission to raise funds for earthquake relief. Gradually, a spark of hope ignited within me, and I felt my energy returning, bit by bit. Still, I was struggling with my own self-image. My self-confidence was shattered, and I found myself complaining and feeling moody. It was a tough battle.

Yet, when I thought of the women enduring oppression worldwide, my determination grew stronger. Women in Iran, Nepal, and beyond deserved better, and I wanted to be a beacon of change.

During a visit with my mother's in Arizona, she surprised me with a birthday cake shaped like Everest, each stage of the climb depicted in sugar-paper images. The cake embodied my unfulfilled dream, a promise to the girls. Tears welled up in my eyes—tears of gratitude mixed with a tinge of sadness. My mother's gesture touched me deeply, yet it also rekindled the pangs of failure within me. "Look at the cake," she urged gently, her voice tender. "You're greater than Everest, and you've already planted your flag on that summit." Her voice quivered, and tears streamed down her cheeks as we embraced.

As we savored the cake at the table, my sister's question pierced the air, breaking the moment. "So, are you going back?" she asked, direct and abrupt.

I hesitated, aware that she anticipated a specific response. "I don't know," I finally admitted, my voice barely audible. "I haven't made a decision yet."

Her eyes flashed with anger, her frustration palpable. "I can't understand how you could be so selfish!" Her words pierced the room. "You put us through so much agony. We thought you were gone!"

Tears flowed freely now, filling the space with raw emotions. It wasn't just about me; there were other crises within the family. My brother faced his own challenges, and his health hung in the balance.

I remained silent, unable to articulate the turmoil within me. Their frustration wasn't solely directed at my endeavors; it was a manifestation of the broader family turmoil. They struggled to comprehend my relentless pursuit of pushing limits and testing boundaries. To many in our community, my focus on helping girls in a distant and unfamiliar country seemed puzzling. "Why not help Iranian girls?" was a common question. "Shouldn't your priority be your own people?"

However, I grappled with the notion of who "my people" were. While I held immense pride in my Iranian heritage, I believed that supporting marginalized girls transcended geographical borders and cultural affiliations.

Amid the pressure from my family to abandon Nepal and mountain climbing, a realization began to crystallize. Maybe, unintentionally, my journey held crucial lessons. Perhaps, beyond scaling the summit, the true message I needed to convey was that pursuing a goal doesn't always result in instant success. Many of our girls faced steep odds, and passing university entrance exams on the first try was often unrealistic. What truly mattered was resilience and unwavering determination, the refusal to surrender in the face of adversity. While another attempt at Everest wasn't on my immediate horizon, I contemplated the profound scrutiny the girls were subjecting me to as they observed how I coped with disappointment.

From then on, whenever confronted with inquiries or criticisms about my risky pursuits or my deviation from traditional expectations, I maintained a stoic silence, nodding in acknowledgment.

It was frequently men from a patriarchal culture who posed the most pointed questions, seemingly threatened by a woman challenging societal norms. "Raising funds for children is commendable," one man conceded, as if his approval was a prerequisite for my endeavors. "But mountain climbing? That needs to stop. Are you trying to harm yourself? What's wrong with you? How can you do this to your husband and family?"

These encounters echoed a recurring theme: that I was deviating from the expected path of a wife and woman. Such sentiments reverberated each time I spoke at different events aimed at fundraising. At one such gathering, I faced three pointed questions: (1) Why not prioritize local girls instead of those Nepali children? (2) Isn't climbing reserved for men? (3) Does your family/husband permit your activities?

Following the earthquake, my primary objective became securing funds to reconstruct residences and schools for young girls. Despite being naturally reserved and introverted, I found myself compelled to engage in numerous conversations and visits. Although this presented a significant challenge, I recognized the necessity of my actions. Similar to the process of preparing for mountain expeditions, the more I dedicated myself to refining my skills as a fundraiser and public speaker, the more my abilities improved. While I once held an aversion to soliciting donations, I gradually realized that the task was not as daunting as I had initially perceived. This shift occurred because I was advocating not for myself, but for those who were in dire need. Receiving negative responses no longer perturbed me; instead, I channeled my focus towards individuals who were willing to extend their assistance.

Chapter 3

Born in Iran

Over 21 years had passed since my family and I left Iran and arrived in the United States amidst a tumultuous period. It often feels like there's a perpetual state of unrest in that part of the world—nations in conflict, religious divisions, and political tensions. We sought refuge in this country, like many immigrants, aiming for a better life and greater opportunities.

During my time as a college student, Iran was undergoing a wave of protests against government restrictions, leading to mass arrests and tragic casualties. I tried to remain inconspicuous, as my family had been waiting for 20 years for a visa to leave the country. I didn't want to jeopardize our chances. The fear of getting into trouble was a constant companion. Although my family wasn't particularly religious, I was repeatedly told at school that a girl must always cover herself to avoid damnation. Gender roles were deeply entrenched, with women needing men's permission for everything, including leaving the country— a dream of mine.

Despite studying electrical engineering at Sharif University, I knew my prospects as a professional were limited. My parents supported my education, hoping it would make me more self-reliant.

My parents constantly fretted over the possibility of me getting apprehended by the morality police on my route to college, all because I refused to completely cover my hair. I despised the notion of being dictated to by someone else, especially the government, regarding my attire and its manner. Despite multiple arrests by the morality police, I remained steadfast in my struggle, determined to demonstrate that they couldn't deprive me of this basic freedom.

Finally, when we were granted permission to leave Iran, I began to envision the freedoms and opportunities America held. While my family settled in Arizona, I set my sights on the University of California, Los Angeles (UCLA) to pursue electrical engineering. The campus felt like a beautiful haven with its diverse student body and high academic standards, but adapting wasn't easy.

I had to start my studies anew, as my previous three years weren't recognized. My English had a British accent, leading to misunderstandings. Cultural norms were different too; a simple gesture of holding hands was misconstrued as something else. Bars and revealing clothing were alien concepts to me. Throughout my time at UCLA, I aimed for excellence, not only to make my family proud but also to create a better life. It was a desire born out of longing for what I couldn't have in Iran—a self-sufficient life, material comforts, and even a family.

After acing final exams, a realization struck me—had I reached my peak? It was like the moment a young champion athlete wonders how to surpass their own success. My mood dipped, and I realized there must be more to life than accomplishments. A feeling of emptiness and depression engulfed me, leading me to realize that I needed to envision grander dreams and set loftier goals for myself.

During one of my classes, my professor pointed out the need for me to enhance my self-confidence. This was because during my presentations, I tended to look at the ceiling instead of maintaining proper eye contact with the audience.

While I excelled in technical subjects, my interpersonal and communication skills needed work. I craved more than just working in a lab on circuit boards, I wanted more in life. The path I walked was unconventional for a girl from Iran, where opportunities were limited. Perhaps that's why I wanted to challenge norms and prove that women were capable of anything. Although I could handle complex technical topics, I recognized the importance of enhancing my interpersonal abilities. Conversations with friends about my self-confidence issue, led me to participate in a communication program called Landmark. I joined the classes to add variety to my life and I was curious to see what would happen.

Opting for science and engineering in my academic pursuits narrowed my exposure to many unexplored facets of life. Hence, it's not surprising that the leadership program I attended to enhance my interpersonal skills had an immediate impact on me. It allowed me to release some lingering resentments and reshape my perspective on certain haunting experiences. As I progressed, I found time to continue my personal growth. I enrolled in another seminar, wherein we were challenged to publicly declare a transformative goal, something immensely ambitious and exciting, pushing the boundaries of imagination.

Initially, my mind drew a blank; I felt stuck. I toyed with the idea of taking up dancing or painting, but they seemed too attainable. Pursuing a Ph.D. in electrical engineering seemed more challenging, yet still within my capabilities. I pondered entrepreneurship, but that had been claimed by others. Money wasn't a strong motivator for me. I owned a car and a modest apartment – I lacked nothing essential.

Considering writing a book crossed my mind, but my experiences weren't noteworthy enough. The concept of opening a wellness center also felt surmountable. I needed a truly exceptional idea.

Suddenly, amidst the conversations around me, inspiration struck. Overhearing discussions about trekking in Nepal, especially to Everest Base Camp, triggered a revelation. I blurted out my goal to climb Mount Everest in a burst of excitement, relishing the attention and approval from the group. Despite never having climbed, hiked, or camped before, I felt empowered by my declaration, even though I feared insects and loathed cold weather.

In addition to my lack of outdoor experience, I had an aversion to cold weather, even in sunny Southern California. Snow was an enigma to me. I owned no suitable gear for this adventure, and my fitness level was far from exceptional. While others might have deemed my goal impossible, I couldn't back down. The room's expectant gazes motivated me to persevere, even though the challenge seemed monumental.

When I announced my plan at the seminar, I received some odd looks, but the reactions from my family and friends were even more unexpected. A friend brushed it off, assuming I was joking, and asked about weekend plans. I was ignored, and he laughed, dismissing my goal as something only affluent individuals pursued. Anticipating the futility of discussing this with my family, I chose to keep it a secret—a skill ingrained in me from an early age.

My family, considered it a passing whim, humoring me rather than challenging my resolve. I couldn't argue, especially after researching that the Everest climb would take two months. The idea of enduring cold weather and being away from home seemed daunting.

My initial online search for guidance yielded a startling fact: roughly one in four people attempting the Everest summit perishes during the endeavor. Numerous bodies remained frozen on the mountain, along with artifacts from failed attempts. Yet, dissuasion was not in my nature; I've been called stubborn before. A similar determination led me to solo travel to Egypt despite dangers, and I had no desire to depend on a man.

My family and friends understood that discouraging me was futile, as it only fueled my determination. Despite my lack of climbing experience, I called a prominent expedition company, Alpine Adventure, seeking advice on how to climb Everest. The guide's inquiry about my previous climbing experience was met with my candid admission that I had none.

Undeterred, I began preparing by seeking guidance at an outdoor store and buying necessary gear. I initiated my training routine, walking on a treadmill with a loaded pack. Overcoming the gym's initial reluctance, I trained rigorously. To form a climbing team, I invited friends, starting with my best friend, Pari. However, my audacious proposal was met with polite refusals.

After persistent attempts, I recruited an experienced climber, Jim, and his friends to join my expedition. Despite mounting doubt, I remained determined. As December arrived, I loaded my pack and embarked on the journey, only to face discomfort and uncertainty at high altitude. Jim's headache and nausea thwarted our progress, forcing us to turn back.

With perseverance, I eventually embarked on my first mountaineering trip in February, determined to reach the summit. However, my companion backed out at the last moment, leaving me to face the challenge alone. I shared my fears with a friend, stressing my commitment and determination.

While recognizing the dangers, I articulated my belief that this was a matter of honor and an important personal goal. Despite attempts to dissuade me, my resolve was unshakable. I embarked on the journey, armed with the leftover food my friend had given me as a parting gift.

On the morning of the ascent, I awoke to find the road to Whitney Portal closed due to heavy snowfall. Undeterred, I continued my journey in my car, despite the slippery conditions, and ended up getting stuck. Stranded in a remote area, my prospects seemed bleak. However, to my astonishment, two strangers appeared seemingly out of nowhere. They inquired about my purpose and, upon learning of my plan to climb Whitney, helped me get my car back on track. It felt as though these unexpected helpers were like guardian angels sent by the universe to offer support.

Upon arriving at the trailhead, a solitary figure in the snowy landscape, I packed my supplies into my backpack, including two liters of water and some leftover pizza and buffalo wings—perhaps unconventional sustenance for such an expedition. As I set out to climb, leg cramps developed early on, possibly a warning to turn back, but I pressed on, determined to prove my resolve.

With each step, I sank into the snow up to my thighs, posing a challenge to my progress. The silence around me was eerie, broken only by the sound of my own labored breath. Despite the obstacles, I persisted, gradually finding a rhythm as I ascended. By the time darkness fell, I managed to reach a suitable campsite, although the cold was becoming increasingly intense.

With the sun hidden behind the mountains, I faced a rapidly darkening landscape. I set up my camp on a slightly inclined flat rock, the only relatively dry spot available. Needing to replenish my water supply to combat altitude sickness, I descended to a frozen lake, using an ice ax to create an opening in the ice for refilling my bottles. I then returned to my camp, placing the bottles at the bottom of my backpack to prevent freezing.

In my quest to stay warm during the night, I discovered a crucial oversight—my sleeping bag had become wet due to a leaking water bottle. Adding to my predicament, I had opted not to bring a tent to save weight in my backpack. Now perched on a rock with a damp sleeping bag, the frigid wind intensified my discomfort. Overwhelmed by fear and cold, I succumbed to tears, feeling a sense of impending doom. My emotions spiraled as I realized the gravity of my situation, fearing that this could be how people met their end in such conditions.

For around 20 minutes, I wept and contemplated the dire circumstances. The biting wind roused me from my stupor, and I crawled into my damp sleeping bag, seeking whatever warmth it could offer. Desperate and shaken, I recorded a video on my phone, my voice barely audible above the howling wind. Reflecting on that recording later, I felt a profound sense of shame at my display of vulnerability and fear.

"I'm so, so sorry. So sorry. I shouldn't have come here. I shouldn't be here alone. Everyone was right. I have no business doing this. Not. . . not. . .just not a good idea. But too late. I wish. . .I wish I didn't do this. I wish. . ." And then it abruptly stopped.

But then a funny thing happened. It's like my brain got plugged back in or something. I could hear this voice talking to me, saying "You don't have to die here."

Suddenly, the knowledge I had absorbed about mountaineering came rushing back to me. "First things first," I resolved, "I need to stop complaining. Then, I should eat something immediately and start moving to generate body heat before it becomes too late." The thought of the buffalo wings and pizza emerged as surprisingly appealing in the chilling isolation atop the remote mountain. Engaging in over two hours of jogging in place became necessary to restore sensation to my numb limbs. However, after a full day of climbing and exhaustion setting in, I had to find a place to rest. Repeatedly urging myself, "Stay awake, don't fall asleep," I knew that succumbing to slumber would spell my demise. My sopping wet sleeping bag in the freezing cold was a lethal combination.

Fatigue must have overpowered me, as around two in the morning, I felt a touch on my bag, eliciting an immediate scream, "It's a bear!" I burrowed deeper into my bag, my head covered, mistakenly believing that I should play dead if it were indeed a bear. Yet, I had forgotten that bears were hibernating at this time. Other thoughts crossed my mind: a potential assailant or even a savior attempting to rescue me. Slowly and cautiously, I peeked outside, discovering a massive snowdrift had accumulated on top of me due to the wind. Fearful of dozing off again, I endured the cold, eagerly awaiting the break of dawn to resume movement.

As the first light pierced the sky, an immense sense of relief washed over me. The feeling was akin to the elation I experienced when I was eventually rescued on Everest two years later. I survived! I'm alive! The fact that I had endured the night was almost incomprehensible. Extracting myself from my frozen sleeping bag, which had solidified into a crust of ice and snow, I quickly gathered my belongings, donned my crampons for traction, and descended as swiftly as I could manage. My haste led to some wrong turns, even getting trapped in waist-deep snow on occasion, necessitating my own rescue efforts. These obstacles, however, paled in comparison to the overwhelming gratitude of being alive.

Upon reaching my car, my sole objective was to descend the mountain as rapidly as possible, yet, predictably, I became stuck once more. Alone and stranded, I found myself in this predicament again. To my surprise, another rescue followed, this time by a couple who casually approached and offered their assistance. Bewildered, I stammered, "Of course," while questioning their presence. Their laughter filled the air as they explained, "We just came up here to check out the snow. Seems like quite a lot." And like ephemeral phantoms, they vanished once more.

That night on Whitney, I confronted my most formidable fears: the dread of solitude, darkness, cold, and above all, death. These apprehensions had always seemed insurmountable, yet I emerged triumphant. While my attempts to reach the summit had fallen short twice, the profound victory lay in my survival. I had proven to myself that I could rely on my own resourcefulness to extricate myself from perilous situations.

While I took pride in my ability to thrive under pressure, a sense of unfinished business lingered regarding conquering the elusive mountain peak. I waited until the spring thaw before finally achieving the summit a few months later. Once I descended, I wasted no time and dialed Alpine Adventure again. This time, when the voice on the other end answered, I declared, "Alright, I did it. I climbed Whitney just like you instructed. What comes after this?"

Unlike before, the guide recognized my earnestness and seriousness about my aspirations. "Well, that's a starting point. Next, you'll need to enroll in some mountaineering courses and master proper techniques."

"Such as?" I inquired, intrigued by what he had in store for me.

"You need to grasp everything! Lives are on the line here. Yours and those of your team members. An oversight or careless mistake imperils not only you but everyone tethered to your rope. We'll teach you about proper techniques, safety protocols, crevasse rescue...," he began.

"Crevasse? What's that?" I interjected.

"It's a deep fissure in a glacier that can seem bottomless. Fall into one of those, and you might end up on the other side of the world."

I chuckled, but he carried on unperturbed. "Then there's route finding, glacier traversal, rope handling, belay techniques, rappelling, crampon usage, rock climbing, and self-arrest."

After each item on the list, I repeated, "I see," masking my further lack of knowledge. Self-arrest sounded like detaining oneself for a crime. Later, I understood it referred to using an ice ax to halt a slide down an icy slope.

"Ah, and one more thing," he added.

"Yes?" Overwhelmed by the information and dreading the phrase "one more thing," I tried to maintain politeness.

"In case you attempt an 8,000-meter peak—that's over 26,000 feet—you'll be responsible for your own pack. On Mt. Rainier, that's around 65 pounds; on Denali in Alaska, much more, about 85 pounds. Understand?"

"Of course," I replied, though uncertainty lingered. "But I weigh just 110 pounds."

"Then you better gain some weight and enhance your training."

"But can someone my size actually do this?"

He skirted the question, leaving me puzzled. Yet, doubt spurred me on. I intensified my training efforts, hiring a personal trainer experienced in preparing mountaineers for summit endeavors. I enrolled in a series of courses as suggested, gradually tackling more challenging climbs. I ventured into the Cascade Mountains in Washington State with a team to hone survival skills and acclimatize to high altitudes. It marked my first encounter with plastic mountaineering boots—bulky, weighty footwear that provided the necessary insulation and support. After the initial day, I counted 12 blisters on my left foot and 11 on my right.

Despite the hardships and inconveniences inherent in such demanding conditions, I swelled with pride over my burgeoning skill set. I grew adept at knot tying, felt empowered during climbs, and discovered that I could easily keep pace with my larger, stronger male counterparts. At the end of the weeklong program, I reached out to Alpine Adventure once again. By now, the staff was familiar with my journey, and we were on a first-name basis. I informed them of my course completion. "So, what's next? When do I get to tackle Everest?"

"Slow down there!" I was cautioned. "You've still got a long way ahead of you."

Chapter 4

Kathmandu

It seems like everything I've undertaken in the mountains up to this point has served as preparation and rehearsal for what I consider the ultimate challenge. Each climb was meticulously chosen to assess and refine a specific skill set: acclimatization, physical conditioning, adapting to freezing temperatures, mastering rappelling, understanding avalanche safety, and various other competencies that I've now not only learned but also honed. Yet, now I stand on the cusp of confronting a colossal endeavor—the enigmatic Cho Oyo, often referred to as the "Turquoise Goddess" by Tibetans. Even the renowned Edmund Hillary was thwarted in his attempt to conquer its summit due to treacherous avalanches and the presence of Chinese military forces in the vicinity. While it might not share the fame of K2 or Everest, Cho Oyo has claimed over fifty lives in the pursuit of its peak.

Undertaking this venture means I'll be separated from my family, for a grueling six weeks, and I can't help but be burdened by guilt over that. However, I can't deny that I'm plagued by nerves. The looming uncertainties of enduring the extreme challenges of an environment above 20,000 feet for such an extended period weigh heavily on my mind.

To cope with my anxiety, I adopted a strategy of significantly intensifying my training routine. Alongside my frequent ascents and descents of Mt. Baldy, I escalated my weightlifting, rowing, yoga, indoor rock climbing, running, swimming, and explored various other exercises. I was well aware that once you surpass an altitude of 7,500 meters, your body's oxygen levels become severely depleted, initiating a process of deterioration. Eating and sleeping become challenging, leading to weight loss. Given my relatively low starting weight, I made a concerted effort to gain as much weight as possible, incorporating eating as part of my training regimen.

My guides and trainers emphasized the importance of fortifying my mental state as much as my physical readiness. Thus, I embarked on a ten-day silent meditation retreat, where the emphasis was on relinquishing cravings and embracing the impermanence of everything. While I may not have fully embraced these concepts, it was constructive practice for my mental resilience.

I was especially eager about my initial stop in Kathmandu, as I would have the opportunity to meet the scholarship girls for the first time. I had coordinated with the staff to inform the children of my arrival before we embarked on our journey into China. I was hoping that my presence as a female mountain climber would be greatly inspiring to them in the face of their challenges. I asked staff regarding what to bring for girls, and they suggested sharing photos of my family and my life to motivate and connect with them. Thus, I carried images from Iran, snapshots of my apartment, my parents and siblings, my gym workouts, and a photo of me holding the Empower Nepali Girls poster before the wind whisked it away on different mountains.

I also found solace in the knowledge that I had virtually met my fellow teammates through social media, discovering their amicable, spirited, and humorous nature. Learning that another woman, Laura, would accompany us further boosted my confidence. Laura aimed to conquer the Seven Summits like Lakpa Sherpa, our guide despite being a mother of six. Impressively, she had already achieved this goal except for Everest, which she had attempted twice before but was forced to turn back each time due to bad weather conditions.

Coincidentally, Laura and I shared the same flight to Kathmandu, granting us an opportunity to connect at the gate. Witnessing her petite stature reassured me that we were in this endeavor together.

First time in Nepal

August 2014, this marked my inaugural journey to Nepal, and I had minimal insight into what lay ahead except for the brief warnings from Dr. Jeffrey Kottler, the founder of nonprofit organization ENG. Upon arrival, the airport presented an unfinished appearance, featuring just a lone building and a solitary runway. I recalled a tale of a grounded plane that stumped mechanics, prompting the manufacturer's intervention. Ultimately, the peculiar solution involved a sacrificial goat on the runway, which astonishingly coaxed the engines back to life.

My initial impression was of a hazy and dusty ambiance accompanied by a sense of organized chaos. Despite my familiarity with the Middle East, Nepal's version of the developing world caught me off guard. The nation seemed to grapple with a constant stream of disruptions—strikes, delays, unruly traffic, power cuts, political instability, and corruption. Yet, the populace exhibited remarkable patience in the face of these challenges. The Nepali people, characterized by their immense generosity, kindness, and hospitality, left an indelible mark on me.

A unique gesture employed by the Nepali involved a gentle rocking of the head, as I had earlier observed with Lakpa Sherpa. Initially, I misconstrued this movement as a negative response to my queries, but I soon learned it could signify affirmation, agreement, or even a flexible "yes."

It predominantly conveyed a message of accommodation and willingness. Their accommodating and amiable nature, complemented by radiant smiles, made the Nepali a delightful and easygoing group. The most enchanting of all customs was the ubiquitous "Namaste" greeting extended by everyone—elderly individuals, shop owners, servers, children, and even infants. Roughly translated, it signifies, "The divine within me recognizes the divine within you," accompanied by hands forming a triangle under the chin, a symbol of reverence. I pondered how much better the world might be if this gesture replaced handshakes.

The drive from the airport resembled a scene from an absurd movie. Traffic lanes were a nebulous concept. Motorcycles zipped past, carrying entire families—father driving, mother seated behind, children precariously positioned, and an infant nestled on the handlebars. Another motorcycle carried a goat on the driver's lap and a cage of chickens attached to the back. The peculiarities felt oddly familiar, reminiscent of my home.

The driver explained that the day's congestion and chaos were exacerbated by an ongoing festival. I inquired if it was a special holiday, while Laura, who had visited Kathmandu before, observed a cow obstructing traffic from the window. I couldn't help but notice armed police or soldiers stationed at various points, hoping their weapons remained unloaded.

Nodding his head in agreement, the driver elaborated, "Yes, it's Teej, a special holiday where women pray to Lord Shiva for their husbands' longevity. Unmarried women also pray to find suitable husbands. They wear red saris adorned with potes—small glass beads that glisten. And they fast throughout the day."

Interjecting, I sought clarification, "So, women fast all day for their husbands' well-being?"

The driver conveyed affirmation through his characteristic head movement.

Absorbing this information, I mused, "Is there a corresponding day for men to honor women and wish them longevity?"

The driver's response was a nonchalant shrug. "No such day exists."

The parallels to my experiences back home in Iran, where women occupy secondary roles, were unmistakable. I pondered how the local populace would perceive Laura and me—two American women scaling their towering peaks. Equally, I contemplated the impressions the scholarship girls would form of me, a woman resembling them yet vehemently opposed to subservience to men or constraining my life to my husband's well-being.

Yak and Yetti Hotel

Upon arriving at the hotel, Laura and I experienced a surprising level of reassurance, a welcome change after enduring a grueling 24 hours confined to airplane seats. Lakpa, accompanied by another guide named Marvin, eagerly greeted us in the lobby. Several other team members who would join us for the expedition were also present. With little time to settle in, the guides swiftly shifted into a business mindset, initiating a comprehensive gear check. Their meticulousness aimed to ensure we possessed every essential item needed for the impending climb. Their diligence stemmed from the awareness that any missing article, potentially life-saving, could lead to dire consequences within the treacherous "death zone" above 8,000 meters, where oxygen levels plummet to less than 40% of sea level. In my case, my climbing pants were deemed inadequate for the sub-zero temperatures we were about to face. Lakpa's boundless generosity shone through as he offered to lend me an extra pair, given that we shared the same size. This gesture of kindness alleviated my worries, especially considering my limited resources following the loss of clothes and equipment during another expedition and not being able to substitute them due to financial constraints.

After unpacking and refreshing ourselves with a shower, Laura and I decided to venture into the nearby tourist hub known as Thamel. This bustling area attracted backpackers, former hippies, and budget-conscious trekkers seeking affordable food, shopping opportunities, and, unfortunately, sketchy drug transactions. Our arrival in Thamel transported me to a scene reminiscent of the 1960s. The streets teemed with predominantly European youth. At every turn, dubious characters attempted to sell us their goods—incense, miniature instruments, and even hashish. I found amusement in the situation, yet Laura was increasingly perturbed by the constant sales pitches. Jeffrey had shared anecdotes of various scams that could unfold, including women with babies who'd ask for assistance buying milk and food, only to return the items to the store once the tourists had left. These cautionary tales resonated with me, given my familiarity with similar schemes in the Middle East. In a way, Thamel felt like a vibrant, chaotic Disneyland.

Thamel aligned perfectly with my preferences—a chaotic and vibrant atmosphere. Pedestrians, vehicles, scooters, bicycles, and tut-tuts jostled for space in the narrow streets that resembled more of alleyways. Shops overflowed with merchandise, their owners vociferously beckoning passersby. The mingling scents of incense and weed wafted through the air, accompanied by the strains of Tibetan and Hindu music blaring from speakers. This enclave offered an array of products, and I thoroughly enjoyed the art of bargaining, although Laura delegated this task to me due to her aversion to it. Having honed my negotiation skills in Tehran, I employed my favored tactic—starting with half the stated price, feigning displeasure at a modest reduction, and theatrically exiting the store, albeit at a languid pace. The merchant's calls urging me to return and the gradual reconciliation process that followed amused me endlessly. It was more about the ritual than the price itself—a tradition I felt both at ease with and entertained by.

Despite being in Nepal for just a few hours, the sense of belonging was palpable. The people resonated with me, and the vibrant atmosphere of activity was invigorating. As Laura and I navigated the labyrinthine alleys, soaking in the sensory tapestry of sights and sounds, we engaged in a lively exchange, comparing our past climbing experiences. Despite her greater familiarity with the domain, I realized that my upbringing and cultural background positioned me to also play a teaching role as we negotiated our way through this captivating puzzle.

First time meeting Nepali Girls

The following morning, I was supposed to go on a guided tour. One of the staff members, Babita, came to pick me up. She was a social work student who juggled her roles as a scholarship recipient and a staff member—effectively overseeing operations alongside the rest of the staff, her friends, and volunteers who collectively contributed to the cause. Now she has her master's degree in psychology and lives with several scholarship girls who lacked alternative housing options.

During our scooter ride, Babita initiated a conversation about familiar Nepali or Indian actresses. This shared topic formed an immediate connection, as my upbringing in Iran had exposed me to Bollywood songs, leading us to sing along together throughout the journey.

Finally, we reached our destination—a place that remained somewhat enigmatic to me. Two imposing blue doors swung open as we got off the scooter. The road we had traversed was rough and rocky, bordered by narrow walls that could only accommodate one scooter at a time. Gazing through the doors, I inferred that we were at the entrance of a school. A long line of children, arranged by age and stature, had formed on either side. The youngest, perhaps just 3 or 4 years old, stood at the forefront. Each child extended their hands, offering flowers, and some draped a khata—a sacred scarf blessed by the Dalai Lama—around my neck. As I walked through this corridor of goodwill, every child greeted me with the words "Namaste" or "Welcome, ma'am." Overwhelmed with emotion, tears of joy streamed down my face. The experience was beyond words—a cascade of honor and affection from children I had never met.

Evidently, the children were informed of my identity and purpose. They recognized me as an engineer and a mountaineer gearing up to conquer Everest. More importantly, they understood that I was a volunteer and fundraiser for the organization that championed their cause—the support of the neediest girls in their school. While I attempted to express my gratitude and appreciation, the overwhelming desire to embrace each child and convey my unwavering commitment tugged at my heart. In that profound moment, it felt as if my entire life was undergoing a transformation, an irreversible shift. Up until that point, my knowledge of these girls and the foundation's work was primarily derived from anecdotes shared by Jeffrey and others. Yet, in that instance, reality enveloped me. The radiant, smiling faces of these girls symbolized a profound dependence on my actions. I am aware that this might sound melodramatic, but had you been there, standing amidst those beaming children, you too would have felt the same. The tears flowed uncontrollably—emotion simply couldn't be contained.

Anticipation hung in the air as all eyes turned towards me, a collective gaze fixed on my presence. It was evident that they were eager to hear a speech or some words from me, their anticipation palpable in the silence that enveloped the space.

Seated in a circle amidst a gathering of scholarship girls, I found myself among a diverse group, ranging from the eldest, around 12 or 13 years old, to the youngest, mere toddlers of 4 or 5. Babita stepped forward to introduce herself, her composed demeanor and sense of authority catching me by surprise. With Babita at the helm, everything was seamlessly orchestrated, and the girls held her in high esteem. She exemplified the very essence of what they aspired to become someday.

I was requested to share my own story with the girls. I delved into my background, hailing from a distant land, elucidating my role as an educator at an American university, my specialization as an electrical engineer and computer scientist. I could perceive a sense of uncertainty in some of the girls' expressions, grappling with the idea of a woman who resembled them engaging in a traditionally male occupation. Subsequently, I unveiled my ambitious plan to elevate awareness about their needs, starting with conquering Cho Oyo, followed by the daunting ascent of Everest. The reaction was a spectrum of astonishment—some jaws dropped, swiftly concealed by slender hands, while others responded with laughter, as if they were caught up in an enchanting fable.

Upon Babita's prompt, the girls embarked on a rather unexpected introduction. They had diligently memorized a basic self-introduction in English. "I am Amita. I study in Class Three," one of the girls would declare. "My parents' names are Amaya and Sunita. I have two brothers, named Sandesh and Sajit." Uttering this meticulously rehearsed script, they cast their gaze downwards, overcome by shyness that caused them to divert their attention to their own feet.

This situation brought back memories of my own shyness during childhood, a time when I was taught to keep a low profile and avoid making direct eye contact, as displaying confidence in front of elders was considered impolite.

I crouched down next to each of them, gently urging, "Look at me. Keep your head up. Be proud of who you are. You're intelligent and capable of achieving great things. I'm here to support you." Even as I spoke these words, a sense of shyness washed over me. I felt overwhelmed, as if I were out of my element. This was uncharted territory; Jeffrey hadn't prepared me for this part.

After the somewhat awkward round of introductions, I began sharing some of the photos I had brought along. However, it seemed like the initial ice had been broken, and they started inquiring about various aspects of my life. They were curious about how I became an engineer, whether girls could pursue such careers in America, and the reasons behind my mountain-climbing aspirations. Babita explained many Nepali people fail to comprehend why tourists travel far and wide to hike mountains. To them, the mountain trails were practical routes between places, not leisure destinations.

The girls, however, showed a keen interest in mountain climbing and my motivations behind it. After a brief pause, I carefully articulated my response, "Well," I began, "unless we challenge ourselves by tackling difficult tasks and confronting fears, we won't truly understand our own potential. Do you grasp what I'm saying?" I noticed heads nodding in agreement. While I initially doubted the extent of their English comprehension, the older girls especially appeared to resonate with my words. "Climbing mountains," I continued, "represents overcoming hardships for me. It's a way to test my own limits."

Once more, the nodding heads and waggling gestures affirmed their understanding and agreement. "Many people have advised me that mountain climbing isn't suitable for a girl. They claim it's too tough and that I should remain at home, tending to my husband and raising children." Their giggles and suppressed laughter suggested they comprehended the underlying message. The circle of girls drew closer, some even vying for a spot on my lap, while others leaned in to listen intently. I yearned for them to recognize that they too could achieve similar feats, that they had the potential to follow their dreams.

Their questions flowed freely. How did I find my way to the United States? What was life like in Iran during my childhood? What was my husband like? How did I manage to pursue engineering studies? What were my impressions of Nepal so far? Their inquisitiveness brought laughter, especially when they discovered I had married at 30 and hadn't yet become a mother. I explained that my focus was on personal goals before marriage and family, an idea that perhaps contrasted with their cultural norms where marriage at a young age was common.

"No rush," I assured them. "It's important to complete your education and establish independence before marriage. This way, you won't rely solely on a man."

A girl, appearing to be around 14 years old, hesitantly joined the conversation, "Excuse me, Ma'am, but my parents want me to marry my cousin. They're pressuring me, and I feel helpless." Her words pierced my heart, leaving me momentarily at a loss for a solution. The weight of their questions was heavy, but I resolved to find a way to address their concerns.

A teacher from the school arrived, carrying a tray of cookies and a thermos of milk tea, a customary gesture of hospitality in Nepal. Famished from the long flight and the time difference, I eagerly consumed the treats before turning back to the girls. "How about a game?" I suggested. "I noticed that during our introductions, you were quite shy. Your voices were barely audible, and the words you shared seemed rehearsed. Let's try this: Stand up in a circle. When I point to you, look me in the eyes and confidently share something about yourself. It can be anything you like, in English or Nepali. Just speak loudly and with confidence."

This improvised game was met with enthusiasm. Whenever I gestured to one of them, they spoke boldly, their voices resonating with newfound assurance. Though I often couldn't decipher their exact words, their excitement was palpable. In that moment, I realized that despite my primary goal of climbing Cho Oyo, I had already achieved something profound in just one day. Nepal felt like home, and my connection with these girls was as fulfilling as any mountaintop triumph.

We snapped "selfies" together, and a group photo captured the shared joy. With reluctance, I bid them farewell, promising to return in six weeks after my mountain ascent.

Before rejoining my fellow climbers awaiting me back at the hotel, Babita treated me to a meal to sample dal bhat for the first time. This national dish, a combination of rice and lentils, often served with curried vegetables, is a staple for Nepalis, constituting their main sustenance twice daily due to its perceived nutritional value and affordability. To put it mildly, acquiring a taste for it requires time.

Babita had thoughtfully organized visits to a few more homes of scholarship recipients, giving me the opportunity to interact with families and witness their living conditions. Our first stop was a modest hut, scarcely larger than a small hotel room. Inside, a young mother, likely in her late teens, tended to her two little girls, aged 3 and 5. When I inquired about the father's whereabouts, the mother simply shrugged. Apparently, he had ventured to an Arabic country in pursuit of work and had vanished without a trace. Whether he met an unfortunate fate or had abandoned his family remained unknown. Such stories were tragically common, with countless Nepali individuals being exported to countries like Qatar and Dubai to engage in labor that locals consider beneath them. These workers, confined to camps and exposed to life-threatening conditions, toil in construction or maintenance roles, enduring 120-degree temperatures daily, all to send remittances home.

We proceeded to another home visit, where we met an 8-year-old scholarship recipient. As we engaged in conversation, she shared her passion for mathematics, prompting me to request a glimpse of her schoolwork. It became evident that this young girl possessed remarkable intelligence, akin to a precious gem tucked away in this modest, isolated abode, bereft of resources. These children perceive the opportunity to attend school and pursue education as a privilege.

During this visit, an intense flashback swept over me, transporting me back to Iran. I was around 10 years old, celebrating the Persian New Year with no school to attend. A knock echoed at our door, and I answered it, my heart racing with surprise. Standing before me were several of my teachers. I stood there, mouth agape, a mix of astonishment and trepidation filling me.

"May we come in?" one of the teachers gently inquired, noting my perplexed expression. I merely nodded, my shyness compelling me to retreat. An array of worries raced through my mind, convincing me that my actions had led to a grave error. I was certain I had committed some grievous offense, given the unusual circumstances of their visit, especially on a holiday.

I was wrong. The teachers visiting my home during the Persian New Year weren't there to admonish me; rather, they sought to convey their appreciation for my commendable academic progress. As we conversed over tea, mirroring the scene unfolding in the humble Nepali hut, they inquired about various aspects of my life—my academic pursuits, preferred subjects, and even details about our residence. The memory of that event surged back to me with unparalleled vividness as I sat in the small hut, evoking the lasting impact it had on me. It was one of those pivotal moments, perhaps the very first, when I recognized the special talent within me, a gift that my teachers were eager to nurture and support. Their encouragement fueled my determination to strive harder.

Now, the roles were reversed. I was the one endeavoring to inspire and uplift a remarkably gifted young girl who had yet to fully recognize her potential. Overwhelmed by emotion, I abruptly excused myself and rushed outside, tears streaming down my face. It was as if the girl's story resonated so profoundly with my own, forging an unbreakable connection between us. In that moment, I realized that I held the power to impact these children's lives, just as my teachers had transformed mine through their unwavering care and guidance.

Upon returning inside, having feigned a need to use the restroom, I regained my composure. Turning to the mother, I expressed my gratitude for her resilience and dedication to her daughter's education. "You must be immensely proud of her intelligence. With your support and the help of all of us, she will achieve remarkable things in her life." I assured her that we would provide a scholarship and the necessary financial backing to enable her daughter to pursue her education, potentially studying fields like engineering or medicine, paralleling my own journey.

Tears welled up in the mother's eyes, her hands forming the familiar gesture of respect. A radiant smile graced her face as she uttered, "Dheri dhanyabahd," expressing heartfelt gratitude for bestowing upon her daughter something she herself had never received. Tenderly, she reached out to clasp my hands.

This poignant exchange repeated itself half a dozen times that afternoon. In each instance, families welcomed me with tea and biscuits. I stepped into homes where five individuals occupied a space akin to a sizable closet, parents and a child often sharing a pallet on the floor for sleep. The makeshift kitchen consisted of a portable stove on the ground. These encounters served as a powerful reminder that I had forfeited any right to complain about my own circumstances.

By the time we returned to the hotel, I was emotionally drained, compounded by the effects of jet lag and the overwhelming intensity of the day. While my fellow team members indulged in leisure activities—shopping, sightseeing, savoring pizza and beer—I had immersed myself in a hidden world, concealed from the view of climbers and trekkers. This experience, however, proved to be the most valuable "training" I could have undertaken in preparation for the upcoming 45 days in the Himalayas. The newfound clarity of my purpose propelled me forward. In moments of adversity, when the urge to quit beckoned, I would conjure the image of these girls and their reliance on me to shed light on their plight. A profound sense of duty had seized me, compelling me to serve as their role model and demonstrate the boundless potential of women.

It struck me as intriguing that my journey had taken me to these remote corners to inspire and assist these children, yet the profound impact they had on me was immeasurable. In visiting their homes and school, with the intention of sharing my plans to aid them, I had inadvertently received a gift in return. I had unearthed a facet of myself that had been missing—an unwavering sense of purpose. The path ahead appeared unmistakably clear, a trajectory I hoped the girls would follow to manifest their aspirations and ambitions. This newfound conviction infused me with gratitude, energy, and an overwhelming sense of contentment. I felt replete and fulfilled, my purpose inextricably linked to theirs.

Chapter 5

Cho Oyu

Before our big climb, my fellow team members and I decided to venture to Swayambhunath, an ancient Tibetan monastery and Buddhist temple situated atop a Kathmandu hill, affording panoramic vistas of the valley below. This temple, renowned for its architectural splendor, millennia-old heritage, and captivating views, also boasts a permanent population—hundreds of ravenous and somewhat territorial monkeys. These creatures, for reasons unbeknownst to me, are revered as sacred beings and are granted considerable autonomy. Consequently, they roam unrestrained, brazenly snatching food from unsuspecting hands, and on occasion, boldly making off with backpacks or cameras held by unsuspecting tourists.

To safeguard our belongings, a few of us formed a protective circle, hoping to deter the monkeys from launching further assaults. Among the ranks were my roommate and tent companion, Laura, and several other members of our diverse international team. The ensemble included Henri from France, Ted from England, Kyle hailing from Virginia, Jiban—the orchestrator of our expedition and master of logistics—and Marvin, our chief guide. This fleeting day of urban exploration marked our sole opportunity to acquaint ourselves with the city before embarking on our arduous mountain expedition. Already, I relished the camaraderie of this eclectic group—each an intriguing and intrepid individual, a stark contrast to the risk-averse and cautious individuals often encountered back in our home countries.

Nepal's south and north borders aren't far apart, less than 100 miles. Getting from Kathmandu to the Chinese border only takes a few dozen miles. But the narrow, dangerous mountain roads are often blocked by landslides or accidents. This can make the journey take days instead of hours. Even though it might seem quick on a map, I didn't expect the many delays we faced when we set off early the next morning.

We encountered a landslide close to the Chinese border. The road was covered by mud and merged with a river. I was feeling sick, so I wanted to get out of the vehicle and stretch. But this time, the road was completely blocked. We had to leave our vehicle, carry our things through the mud, and repack everything in another vehicle. It surprised me that our guides were so calm about it, as if this happened often—which I guess it does. I started complaining about the mud and the heat until I learned that over 200 people died when a nearby village was buried by the mountain. It reminded me to slow down and be patient, like the Nepalis.

When we reached the border, things were different on each side of the bridge. On the Nepal side, the guards were relaxed and joking around. But on the other side, the Chinese soldiers were serious and well-equipped. They asked for our documents and searched our belongings for forbidden items. One soldier asked about books, and I didn't know how to answer. I had books with me for the long stay in the mountains, but I didn't want to give them up. They checked us thoroughly, even our temperature. It was more intense than a doctor's visit.

The Chinese took some of our food and gear, maybe so we would buy more things from them. I wondered if I would see my own stuff for sale later. We were at a high altitude, but the landscape looked like the desert. Trees and waterfalls were gone. In the next village, we were warned about wild dogs and saw locals smoking. There were other climbing teams too.

I felt uneasy without communication to the outside world—no Internet, email, or news. The motel's TV only had one channel showing a talent show from China. We were isolated. While looking for Wi-Fi, I noticed a big hairy creature following me. It turned out to be a yak, my first sighting.

Yaks are well adapted to living in harsh and high-altitude environments. They have a thick coat of fur to keep them warm and are often used by local communities for their milk, meat, fur, and as pack animals to carry heavy loads in the rugged terrain. Yaks have distinct curved horns and a hump-like feature on their backs. They are important to the people in these areas for various purposes and are often seen as symbols of the region's culture and way of life.

Getting acclimatized is one of the most crucial aspects of training for high-altitude mountain expeditions. This process involves gradually adjusting your body to the reduced oxygen levels found at higher elevations. By spending time at increasing altitudes before attempting the summit, climbers allow their bodies to adapt and build tolerance to the lower oxygen levels. This helps reduce the risk of altitude sickness and other potential health issues that can arise when ascending to extreme heights. Acclimatization hikes and progressively reaching higher altitudes during training are key components of this preparation, ensuring that climbers are better equipped to handle the challenges of high-altitude environments.

Every day we went on hikes to higher places to get used to the altitude. During these walks, I got to know my group members better. Some of the men were much taller and bigger than me, so I had to keep up with their longer steps during climbs. But I quickly realized we would take care of each other.

We heard interesting stories during the climb that helped make the hard times feel a bit easier. Our guides had climbed many tall mountains all around the world, guiding rich clients and adventurous people. They told us about a man in his 60s who fell in love with a 20-year-old and decided to divorce his wife during the trip. Another rich man was worried about his heart, so he flew back to the U.S. to see his heart doctor while he was on Everest. When he found out his heart was fine, he flew back to Nepal and even hired a helicopter to get back to Everest Base Camp. That's quite a quick trip from sea level to 18,000 feet!

We went to the next village, which was even higher, and it was strange too. This time we had to watch out for kids who asked for money. If we didn't give them something, they would kick us or throw things. It got unsafe to be alone, so we had to stay in groups to protect ourselves.

Our routine as we climbed higher towards base camp was pretty much the same every day. We hiked a lot, then came back down and sat by the stove to dry our socks. We had a lot of time to think about life, our priorities, loved ones, and more. But climbing like this is different. In my home, people are always busy with work and responsibilities. We rarely just hang out without TVs or phones. In the teahouses, there was nothing to do but talk to each other about our lives, past adventures, and future plans. In those talks, I shared why I was climbing, not just for Everest preparation, but to show our girls what's possible when you work hard enough.

Camp One, Cho Oyu

I thought BC would be like a village of climbers, but it looked more like an army camp with Chinese soldiers. They told us not to take pictures, but we didn't pay much attention to them. I told my team that I am not sure if I will ever come back here so I better take as many pictures as possible!

Base Camp was a place for us to rest and get used to the high altitude. We had a lot of free time, and since we were all living close together in tents, we talked a lot and we asked each other questions about our lives.

We did a lot of acclimatization hikes! Honestly, I have a unique way of climbing. I enjoy listening to music, especially Persian songs. They're so catchy that I end up dancing as I walk. I swing my arms and move my feet to the beat, even though it's a bit awkward with my heavy gear.

On our way up to Advance Base Camp(ABC), at 17000 feet, we stopped at a teahouse that was more like a small hut covered with tent fabric. The person taking care of the place had a child on her lap. Her husband or brother approached me and asked if I was married and had kids. Then he surprised me by asking if I wanted to take their child to the U.S. I didn't know if he was joking, but it made me uncomfortable. The place smelled bad because they used yak dung for fuel. It was so cold outside that we had to stay inside despite the smell.

As we headed to ABC, our guide Marvin checked on each of us. He asked how I was doing, and I didn't want to lie, so I said my kidneys felt a bit sore. He got angry and said it was because I wasn't drinking enough water. I felt hurt and embarrassed. He said I wouldn't go to the top unless I drank more water.

Later, we reached ABC in a blizzard. The snow was falling heavily, and the wind was incredibly strong. The wind was so forceful that it made my clothes wet, and I was shivering from the cold. I bundled up in all my wet warm clothes but was still freezing. Another team invited us to their tent to warm up. A woman named Christina from the other team was curious about me and what I was doing. When I told her about supporting girls and climbing to raise money for them, everyone was so interested to know more about ENG.

My goal for that day was to drink a lot of water and show Marvin that I was following his advice. He frequently asked me how much water I had drunk, and I proudly told him I had finished nearly two liters. He smiled and gave me a high-five. I could see that he cared about my well-being. If that made him happy, it was no problem for me. However, I noticed that Lakpa Sherpa, seemed different. He wasn't his usual cheerful self; there was something bothering him. I wondered who takes care of him, considering how much he looks after everyone else.

I don't know if it was the high altitude or the fact that we had a relatively easy day, but I didn't have any appetite for dinner. On top of that, I developed a severe headache that prevented me from sleeping. The next day during our acclimatization hike, I felt terrible. My headache worsened, and I had no energy to walk properly. Drinking plenty of water didn't seem to help.

When we got back to ABC camp after a whole day of acclimatization hike, I went straight into my tent and started crying. If the previous days felt like a heavenly experience, this day was like hell. It was the first time I thought I wanted to give up and go home. I felt weak and couldn't bear the pain in my head. I also sensed a sore throat coming on. I felt sick and had no appetite at all. I struggled to remember what I had eaten that day; my head was pounding so hard that I could hardly recall where I was, let alone why I was there.

"A thousand times bigger." I repeated this mantra to myself. It was a reminder that I wasn't climbing for myself but for the girls I wanted to support. I told myself that this suffering was just a minor inconvenience compared to my purpose. However, it was easier said than believed. The reality was that everything up here was incredibly tough. Basic things like using the bathroom, eating, changing clothes, or finding things in my bag were unbelievably challenging and tiring. Everyday tasks that I took for granted back home became exhausting on the mountain. Lying in my tent, feeling sorry for myself and frustrated by the situation, I eventually fell asleep while listening to music at a low volume to avoid worsening my headache.

The next morning, I felt a bit better even though I hadn't slept much. My headache wasn't as bad, but I still felt a dull pressure. I wasn't sure if I was getting better or just getting used to the discomfort.

We were getting ready for serious climbing, so we had a special ceremony called Puja. In this ceremony, we asked the gods for a safe journey. This is a tradition of the Sherpa people, especially those who are monks. Sometimes, the oldest son in a family becomes a monk when they're young to learn about religion and help the spiritual leader, called a lama. If the family is struggling with money, the monk might be allowed to work as a guide to help the family. Some Sherpas in our group led this ceremony.

We had a small altar with colorful flags. While the monks chanted prayers, we put our climbing tools, like crampons and ice axes, on the rocks to bless them for the climb. I also put the Empower Nepali Girls flag there so everyone could see it. We gave symbolic gifts to different gods - Hindu, Buddhist, Christian, Muslim, and others. We burned incense and threw rice as an offering. At the end of the ceremony, we even rubbed flour on each other's faces for a personal blessing. We found this part funny because we looked like ghosts.

Rubbing flour on the face is often considered a form of purification and blessing in many cultures, including Sherpa culture. The flour used in the ceremony is typically made from barley or other grains, and it carries spiritual importance. The act of applying flour to the face is believed to cleanse and purify the climbers, both physically and spiritually, before they begin their journey.

Additionally, the application of flour might symbolize a transformation or a shedding of one's worldly identity as they prepare to face the challenges of the climb. It can also serve as a way to connect with the divine, inviting blessings and protection for the climbers throughout their expedition.

Watching the ceremony made me realize that it wasn't just about climbing or trying to avoid danger with superstitions. It was a ritual to show respect for the mountain, think about the uncertainties in life, and reflect on what our actions mean.

A Challenging Climb to Camp Two

Today, we were carrying our things to Camp One, which is at a height of 21,000 feet. My plan was to leave most of my stuff in my tent to make my backpack lighter. My backpack was already way too heavy, and I couldn't carry it comfortably. It took us 10 hours to go up there and come back to ABC, and it was snowing the whole time.

In the last hour before we reached Camp One, I started regretting my decision to lighten my backpack. I was freezing because I didn't have enough warm clothes. I even thought about giving up on reaching the summit and just going back down. I kept asking myself, "Why are you doing this? Go back down." With each step, I tried to convince myself to take one more step before turning around.

I was so tired that at one point, I felt a sudden jolt and realized I had fallen asleep while walking! This was dangerous because there were deep cracks in the ice, and one misstep could take me down. I was really worried because as we went higher, the slopes got steeper, and the dangers increased.

In my tired state, I started thinking about Diana Nyad. She swam from Cuba to Florida, which was a 110-mile swim that took around 50 hours. She faced big waves, strong winds, jellyfish stings, the fear of sharks, and had to keep swimming for two days straight. She became my inspiration, and I imagined her watching me and encouraging me. I could almost hear her telling me to keep going and reminding me that this goal was bigger than myself. She said, "Remember why you're doing this. It's not just about you. It's for others. Remember the people who believe in you."

Diana Nyad's accomplishment at the age of 64 showcased her incredible endurance, resilience, and spirit of adventure. Her achievement inspired me and emphasized the power of determination and perseverance. She was a symbol of pushing the boundaries of human capability and achieving seemingly impossible goals.

As much as her words helped, the feeling of inspiration didn't last very long. I still thought about giving up. Then I remembered how amazing it felt when I reached the summit of Aconcagua. It wasn't as tough as this challenge, but it reminded me why I was pushing myself. Somehow, I held onto that feeling until we finally reached the high camp.

After coming down from that initial climb to Camp One, we were given a day to rest and recover, and let me tell you, we really needed it. Almost everyone had headaches, sore throats, and felt like they had the flu. When I struggled to reach 21,000 feet, I couldn't help but wonder how I would manage another 6,000 feet. Honestly, at that moment, if I had the energy to leave my tent, I might have tried to find Marvin or Lakpa and ask for help to get back down. But I was too tired to do anything, so I just stayed in my tent, feeling terrible and hoping I could fall asleep.

During the night, I got out of my sleeping bag, forgetting that I had thought about giving up the day before. This time, it wasn't because I was tired, in pain, or because of the high altitude. I had left some of my things, including my pee bottle, at Camp One. I use that bottle at night so I don't have to go outside in the cold. I remembered Laura saying that holding in your pee lowers your body temperature. But I had to drink a lot of water, so I couldn't hold it until morning. I had to go out at around 2 AM. When I stepped outside the tent, I saw the most amazing view - the sky was full of bright stars. It was so beautiful that I almost forgot why I was outside, until I remembered I needed to pee.

By then, I was freezing from being outside, and I didn't really want to take off my pants. I thought about going back inside and waiting until morning, but my stomach hurt so much and I had diarrhea. I had no choice but to deal with it. I also knew I had to sleep because we were going back to Camp One the next morning, and that would be our new base. I was actually looking forward to it because I would be sharing a tent with Laura again. I didn't like being alone.

As I lay there, waiting to fall asleep, I started thinking about all the things I had learned over the years about staying positive, especially when things are tough. Climbing mountains is not just physical, it's mental too. It's about handling problems without getting discouraged. It's about staying focused and disciplined. But most importantly, it's about staying positive, especially when things get really, really hard. I realized that if I could make it to the summit, anything else I faced in life back home would be much easier.

It was strange how my feelings changed so quickly and unexpectedly. One moment, I felt like giving up, and the next, I felt fearless. I was amazed by the stars one minute, and then I was crying and feeling miserable. I needed to stay more balanced and not get upset by every little problem. I needed to keep positive thoughts flowing, so I practiced my meditation to relax and clear my mind. The next thing I knew, it was morning, and I had slept really well. I felt renewed and full of energy. My cramps, nausea, and headache were all gone.

The experiences I gain while climbing teach me resilience, patience, and the importance of staying positive in tough situations. It's not just about the physical journey; it's also about the mental and emotional growth that comes from facing difficult moments.

I carry the knowledge from these mountains with me, and it guides me in my daily life. It reminds me that no matter how tough things seem, they will eventually pass. Just like the challenges of climbing, every obstacle in life is temporary, and with the right mindset, I can overcome them. Mountains have become my source of inspiration and wisdom, shaping me into a stronger and more enriched individual.

On Our Way To the Summit of Cho-Oyu

After a few difficult days we reached Camp Three, and I rediscovered my passion and excitement. I guess my body was acclimatizing better. The day was amazing, clear and chilly. I could see snow-covered peaks all around, rising above the valley below.

At high altitude, as the sun begins its descent towards the horizon, the world undergoes a breathtaking transformation. The sky becomes a canvas of vibrant hues, transitioning from a soft blue to a rich tapestry of colors. The first hints of pink and orange start to paint the heavens, casting a warm glow across the snow-covered peaks.

As the sun continues to lower, the colors intensify, turning the sky into a masterpiece of gold, magenta, and crimson. The snow-capped peaks catch fire with radiant light, as if they're ignited from within. The snow that blankets the mountains reflects the colors of the sunset, creating an otherworldly scene where nature's elements collaborate to create an ethereal spectacle.

The sunlight dances upon the icy surfaces, causing them to sparkle and shimmer like a field of diamonds. The shadows cast by the rugged terrain become long and dramatic, adding depth and dimension to the landscape. It's a fleeting moment of unparalleled beauty, where time seems to stand still, and the world around you is bathed in a soft, enchanting glow.

The hues gradually deepen as the sun sinks lower, and the atmosphere becomes awash with a tranquil palette of purples and indigos. The snow peaks, now enveloped in these cool shades, exude an air of serenity and mystery. The transition from day to night is accompanied by a sense of awe and wonder, as the mountain landscape transforms into a realm of dreams and magic.

In this rare and captivating moment, the high-altitude mountain is not merely a physical entity; it becomes a living, breathing entity that resonates with the colors of the universe. The sunset paints a vivid story on the canvas of nature, leaving an indelible mark on the hearts of those fortunate enough to witness this celestial masterpiece.

We were so high up, higher than I had ever been, not just in terms of height but also in my spirit and emotions. I felt joyful and pure. I also felt strong and confident for our early morning summit attempt.

All the worries and frustrations from earlier days seemed to disappear. Even my wet socks had dried, and even though my feet smelled bad when I took off my boots, it couldn't ruin my happy mood.

After the sunset, we tried to eat, and then went to our tents to rest before our wake-up call around 11 PM. Laura and I were too excited to sleep, so we lay quietly and listened to each other breathe, which was comforting.

The summit attempt is a remarkable endeavor that begins long before dawn, when we rouse from our slumber and the stars shimmer above. In the heart of the night, well before the first rays of light, we awaken to a symphony of rustling sleeping bags and quiet murmurs. The camp is alive with a shared purpose, a collective resolve to conquer the peak that looms in the distance. With headlamps casting a pale glow, we set about our preparations.

Amid the chilly air, we don our gear, layering ourselves in insulated clothing to fend off the biting cold. Each piece of equipment is checked and double-checked in the dim light, ensuring that nothing is overlooked. Nervous excitement courses through our veins as we tighten our boots, adjust our gloves, and fasten our helmets.

A modest meal is consumed, a humble sustenance that will provide the energy needed for the arduous ascent. High-energy snacks, warm drinks, and calorie-dense foods are carefully selected, offering a brief reprieve from the chill and a promise of the strength to come.

We gathered together, a united team bound by a shared goal. We exchange glances, perhaps offer a few words of encouragement, and then step into the inky blackness. Headlamps create a tunnel of light, guiding our way up the winding path. Footsteps fall in rhythm, a synchronized dance of determination as we navigate the rocky terrain and winding trails.

As we ascend, the darkness begins to yield, and a soft illumination paints the landscape. The first hints of dawn slowly creep over the horizon, unveiling the contours of the mountain and revealing the breathtaking beauty that surrounds us. The sky transforms from velvety black to shades of deep blue and rosy pink, a celestial transition that mirrors our own journey.

With each step, the air becomes thinner, and the effort required intensifies. Yet, I have to persist, driven by an unrelenting desire to reach the summit. The path became steeper, the cold more biting, and the winds more insistent. I draw upon all my inner reservoirs of strength, mentally and physically pushing forward despite the challenges.

As we ascend higher, the first rays of sunlight pierce the sky, casting a warm and golden hue across the landscape. The world seems to quietly awaken with us, bathed in the soft light of a new day. With hearts pounding and breath visible in the cold air, I press on, my determination unwavering.

With every step, the summit grows closer, a beacon of triumph and accomplishment. As we near the top, our fatigue is overshadowed by the exhilaration of our achievement. The final push becomes a testament to our endurance, a culmination of months of preparation and the culmination of countless challenges.

And then, with a mixture of exhaustion and elation, we stood at the summit. Unbelievable! The world stretched out before us, a breathtaking panorama that defied description. We've conquered not only the physical demands of the climb but also the mental and emotional hurdles that came with it. The beauty that surrounds us is a reward that transcends words, a testament to our dedication and the sheer willpower that propelled us to this moment.

In that quiet, windswept space atop the world, I found a profound sense of a connection to something greater than myself. We navigated the dark hours of the night and ascended to the pinnacle of the mountain, a place where the challenges of the journey below fade into insignificance. With a mixture of pride and humility, I took in the view, a testament to our indomitable spirit and the power of human determination.

What caught my attention as we reached the top was majestic Everest, even higher. Next to it was Lhotse, almost at my eye level. I turned and saw prayer flags fluttering in the wind. I can't describe the feeling of accomplishment in doing something so hard, wanting to give up many times but pushing through. Two years ago, I had never been in the mountains, and there I was, at 27,000 feet. It was like an unbelievable experience, almost like I was weightless. I was so grateful for the chance to go through this, no matter how tough it had been to get here.

Once you reach the top of a tall Himalayan mountain, you can't celebrate for long. It's as high as airplanes fly in the sky's fast stream of air. It's super cold, like 30 degrees below freezing. The wind is really strong, blowing at 50 miles per hour. You only have a few minutes at best to enjoy the moment before you have to leave to stay safe.

I took out a banner for Empower Nepali Girls that I had been carrying. I held it between my arms to take a picture. I wanted to show the girls back in Kathmandu and the villages. I asked Lakpa Sherpa, to take a photo of me.

Standing at the summit, a mix of exhilaration and discomfort washed over me. The bitter cold bit into my fingers and toes, numbing them to the point where I could hardly feel them at all. Each breath was a struggle, the thin air making it difficult to fill my lungs.

In my eagerness to capture the moment, I had lifted my oxygen mask to take pictures. It seemed like a small concession at the time, but it proved to be a critical error. The freezing temperatures caused the mask to freeze, rendering it useless for the descent. As I prepared to make my way down the mountain, the realization struck me: I would have to navigate the treacherous path without the assistance of oxygen, a vital lifeline in such high altitudes.

The breathtaking scenery before me seemed to contrast sharply with the physical discomfort I was experiencing. Majestic peaks stretched into the distance, an awe-inspiring panorama that spoke of the enormity of nature's grandeur. Yet, I couldn't escape the biting cold that seemed to pierce through every layer of clothing.

I tried to use my camera to take pictures of the amazing views, but it was frozen and the battery was dead. Luckily, I kept my phone warm inside my jacket, and it still had full battery. But even that died after taking a few photos. It's okay though, I tried my best to remember everything. Sometimes, taking photos can make you remember less because your brain knows the picture has the memory. So, I looked around in awe, trying to remember these special moments for which I had worked so hard to achieve. Honestly, the whole scene was so incredibly amazing that it felt unreal.

As I gazed out at the expansive view, I couldn't help but reflect on the journey that had brought me here. The sacrifice, the effort, and the unwavering belief in the possibility of reaching this lofty goal. The discomfort I felt in that moment was a stark reminder of the price of such achievement, a reminder that the pursuit of greatness often comes with its own set of challenges.

With a mixture of pride and determination, I braced myself for the descent. The journey was far from over, and the path ahead would test my mettle once again. But as I took a final look at the breathtaking landscape that surrounded me, I carried with me the memory of that summit moment, a testament to the heights we can reach when we push beyond our limits.

Chapter 6

Firs Iranian 7 Summitter

I began the first chapter of this book by sharing my experiences during the earthquake in 2015. It was a significant event in my story for a while. However, in 2016, I published my first book and poured my heart into it. I also sought therapy to address the trauma I had from the earthquake and avalanche. During this time, I made a powerful decision: I announced to the Nepali girls that I intended to return and climb Mount Everest once again. But my goal wasn't just Everest; it was to conquer the Seven Summits—the highest peaks on each of the seven continents. This ambitious endeavor was tied to seven nonprofit organizations dedicated to empowering women.

My purpose was clear—I didn't want to show the girls the path of giving up. Instead, I aimed to teach them that when life throws challenge your way, you must rise, persevere, and remain resilient. This determination guided me through the following chapters, where I'll share my experiences returning to Everest on multiple occasions. I'll recount the hurdles, the victories, and the eventual triumph of reaching the summit on May 20th, 2022. But the journey doesn't stop there. I'll also delve into the tales of conquering the other six summits, each linked to a unique nonprofit organization that I collaborated with to raise funds and awareness.

So, here we go—a story of resilience, determination, and the unyielding spirit to make a positive impact, one summit at a time.

The realization struck me: among all the incredible mountain climbers and athletes in Iran, no other Iranians had conquered the Seven Summits. This fact resonated deeply within me. I saw an opportunity—a chance to undertake this monumental feat on behalf of my entire nation, particularly the 40 million women facing oppression and unequal opportunities.

Growing up in Iran, I often felt like a second-class citizen. The idea of embarking on this audacious journey held a special significance. I yearned to inspire my fellow Iranian women, offering them a beacon of hope in a country where oppression was a harsh reality. The weight of the regime's actions, which included the unjust killing of innocent people to maintain power, fueled my determination to do something extraordinary.

Recent events, such as the protests and the women's freedom movement in Iran, served as a powerful reminder of the resilience and strength within us. The courage displayed by those who stood up against the oppressive regime further solidified my commitment to empowering women. I understood that empowering and educating women could catalyze positive change, benefiting not only the individual lives but also the entire nation's economy.

The question that persisted in my mind was why so many Middle Eastern countries sought to suppress their women. It was a perplexing and troubling reality. Despite the proven advantages of empowering women, certain nations continued to deny them equal opportunities and basic rights. The why behind this oppressive approach remained an enigma.

In the face of these challenges, my determination grew stronger. I was resolute in my mission to climb the Seven Summits and advocate for the empowerment of Iranian women. I believed that my journey, my triumphs, and my advocacy could ignite a spark of hope and change within my country. Through my actions, I aimed to demonstrate that even in the face of adversity, we could rise, empower ourselves, and create a brighter future.

I have vivid memories from my childhood. Whenever I wanted to play soccer or climb trees, they would tell me, "You're a girl, you shouldn't do that. Go play with dolls like your sisters." Even when I wanted to join biking competitions or play as a forward in soccer, they insisted I be a goalie. I saw women around me denied their rights and held back from reaching their potential. These experiences left a mark on me.

In 2002, my family and I moved to the US, and I was excited about the newfound freedom to pursue my passions. However, the voices that had been planted in my head continued to hold me back. They whispered that I shouldn't do certain things because of my gender. These doubts persisted even as I got married. Balancing between being myself and fulfilling the role of a "good" wife, focused on cooking, cleaning, and household tasks, was a challenge.

I believe many who have faced similar struggles, leading to divorce due to the inability to be true to oneself, can empathize with my journey. It became clear that I needed to break free from these limitations to fully grow and take charge of my own happiness and well-being. Ultimately, I had to undergo a divorce to embrace my personal growth and independence, and to no longer rely on others for my fulfillment.

I'll delve into more personal life details in the upcoming chapters, but let's return to my journey of conquering the Seven Summits.

As I reflect on my experiences, it's important to note that being single granted me extra time and freedom to pursue my passion for travel and high-altitude mountain climbing. When it comes to tackling an 8000-meter mountain, such as the ones in the Seven Summits challenge, it requires a substantial amount of time— usually around 6 to 8 weeks of climbing, not to mention the months of preparation and training beforehand.

In this context, my single status and lack of children played a crucial role. It provided me with the flexibility needed for extensive training and the demanding climbing schedules that come with such monumental goals. This freedom allowed me to focus wholeheartedly on honing my skills, building my strength, and preparing myself both mentally and physically for each ascent.

It's worth highlighting that high-altitude climbing demands a significant commitment. The combination of training, acclimatization, and the actual climb itself is a rigorous process that requires dedication and focus. Being single provided me with the opportunity to fully immerse myself in this pursuit, without the added responsibilities and time constraints that come with a family.

As I share my journey, I hope it becomes clear how this particular life circumstance facilitated my pursuit of the Seven Summits and enabled me to strive for these awe-inspiring accomplishments.

In contrast, my journey was also enriched by the presence of remarkable mothers who shared my tent. These incredible women, each with 4, 5, or even 6 children, had scaled the world's highest peaks. Their accomplishments served as a beacon of inspiration for mothers everywhere, showcasing that the responsibilities of parenthood need not hinder one's ability to pursue mountain climbing and other extraordinary achievements.

Their presence emphasized a valuable lesson: being a parent doesn't have to limit your ambitions or passions. These moms demonstrated that with determination, support, and effective time management, it's entirely possible to balance the demands of raising a family with the pursuit of high-altitude climbing. Their stories highlight that parenthood doesn't need to be an obstacle; instead, it can be a source of strength and motivation.

I share this to provide a well-rounded view of where I was in my own journey. While my single status afforded me a particular advantage in terms of time and flexibility, the experiences of these incredible moms underscore the power of resilience and the potential to achieve greatness even amidst the responsibilities of motherhood.

Before moving forward with my journey, it's essential for me to share a significant chapter of my life. In 2018, I faced the decision to get divorced. This choice was driven by a need for personal space and time to process the complexities of the past 15 years in a relationship. It was a period of introspection, healing, and contemplation about the path ahead.

After the divorce, I realized the importance of taking time for myself. This period of solitude allowed me to reflect on my experiences, understand my emotions, and envision my future. I embarked on a journey of self-discovery, seeking answers to questions about my identity, aspirations, and purpose. Central to this process was finding closure with my past, embracing forgiveness, and ultimately attaining a sense of completeness.

In essence, this phase was an essential chapter in my life that paved the way for the adventures and challenges I would go on to face. It was a time of personal growth, transformation, and renewal, marking the beginning of a new chapter that would lead me to greater heights—both figuratively and literally.

Nature Time for Thinking & Reflection

I summitted most of the 7 summits on my period. Mountain climbing presents unique challenges for women, encompassing a range of physical and practical considerations. From managing menstrual cycles to navigating the potential risks associated with certain birth control methods, the journey is marked by distinct hurdles. Privacy during moments like urination can be particularly challenging, underscoring the importance of a supportive and understanding team.

Menstrual cycles, a natural part of a woman's reproductive health, can coincide with climbing expeditions. The physical and emotional effects of menstruation can impact energy levels, mood, and overall well-being. Climbing at high altitudes intensifies these challenges, as altitude sickness, fatigue, and dehydration can exacerbate menstrual symptoms. Furthermore, managing hygiene and discomfort in remote and rugged environments becomes a crucial concern.

Addressing menstruation involves thoughtful preparation. I had to carry sufficient sanitary supplies, ensure proper waste disposal in eco-sensitive areas, and manage hygiene to prevent infections. Being mentally and physically prepared for the effects of menstruation on climbing performance is essential. Adaptations in climbing strategies, rest periods, and nutrition may be necessary to navigate the fluctuations in energy and stamina.

Regarding birth control, climbers often face choices between methods that suit their individual needs while considering potential risks associated with altitude and physical exertion. Some birth control methods, such as hormonal contraceptives, may increase the risk of blood clots, which can be exacerbated by high-altitude conditions.

In both cases, open communication within climbing teams is pivotal. A supportive team fosters an environment where climbers can openly discuss their needs, concerns, and experiences. Understanding and empathy from teammates can alleviate the stress and discomfort associated with these aspects of climbing.

Chapter 7

1st Summit: Aconcagua

Climbing Aconcagua was an exhilarating yet demanding experience that tested my limits and determination like never before. As I embarked on this journey, I knew that conquering the highest peak in South America would be no small feat. The challenges and rewards that awaited me were both exciting and nerve-wracking.

The ascent of Aconcagua is a multi-day endeavor, characterized by a series of well-defined camps that mark the stages of the climb. Each camp brings its own set of challenges and adjustments, creating a gradual progression toward the summit.

The base camp, Plaza de Mulas, was the starting point of this adventure. Nestled at an altitude of around 14,000 feet, it served as our initial acclimatization hub. As I set foot in this bustling camp, I was greeted by a buzz of activity—fellow climbers from around the world, porters, and guides preparing for the ascent ahead. The sense of camaraderie was palpable, as we all shared the same goal of reaching the summit.

Moving higher, we transitioned to Camp One, Plaza Canada, perched at approximately 16,000 feet. The thin air and rugged terrain began to take its toll, making each step a bit more arduous. At this point, acclimatization was key, and our daily routines revolved around short hikes to higher altitudes, then returning to lower camps for rest. The beauty of the surrounding landscape was awe-inspiring, with jagged peaks and expansive glaciers stretching as far as the eye could see.

Camp Two, Nido de Condores, situated around 18,000 feet, presented a new set of challenges. The air grew thinner, and even simple tasks felt like significant efforts. Adapting to these conditions required patience and a strong mindset. As I laid down in my tent at night, I could feel the altitude's impact on my body—a constant reminder of the heights I was reaching.

Climbing to Camp Three, Berlin, at approximately 19,000 feet was a true test of endurance. The gradient steepened, and my steps grew slower and more deliberate. The thin air meant that even the simplest tasks left me breathless. Yet, the sight of the surrounding Andean peaks was an awe-inspiring reward that fueled my determination.

Approaching the final stretch, we pushed to Camp Four, Colera, situated around 20,000 feet. The atmosphere was noticeably thinner, and the temperatures plummeted. This camp marked the launching point for our summit push. We prepared for a midnight start, bundled up in layers of clothing to brave the frigid conditions. The anticipation and excitement in the air were tangible, as climbers from various teams converged for the final ascent.

The summit day was a blend of sheer determination and awe-inspiring vistas. The climb became more mentally demanding as the air grew thinner, but each step brought me closer to my goal. As dawn broke over the Andes, the horizon was painted in hues of gold and pink—a breathtaking sight that rejuvenated my spirits. The final push to the summit was both physically and emotionally exhausting, but the exhilaration of reaching the top was beyond words.

When our guide, Mario, uttered the words that we were just minutes away from the summit, a rush of emotions overcame me, and tears welled up in my eyes. The sheer joy and disbelief washed over me like a tidal wave. This was an indescribable moment, as it marked not only the culmination of our ascent but also a significant personal milestone.

The enormity of the achievement hit me with full force. This was my first time ascending to such remarkable heights, and the realization of how far I had come filled me with an overwhelming sense of happiness. The fact that I was standing on the brink of reaching the summit of Aconcagua, a towering peak that had challenged me every step of the way, was a testament to my dedication and perseverance.

As the tears streamed down my cheeks, a surge of confidence coursed through me. This moment was more than just a physical feat; it was a transformative experience that expanded my horizons and bolstered my self-belief. The challenges I had surmounted during the climb had fortified my spirit, and now, gazing at the final stretch to the summit, I felt an unshakable assurance that I could conquer even greater heights in the future.

The summit of Aconcagua became a symbol of possibility, a beacon of hope that illuminated the path for my future climbs. It was a validation of my aspirations, a reminder that with determination, dedication, and the support of a skilled guide like Mario and a steadfast team, no peak was insurmountable. The tears that flowed down my face were a manifestation of the overwhelming joy, gratitude, and triumph that defined that pivotal moment.

Tragically, a few years later, Mario's journey came to an untimely end while climbing a challenging mountain in Pakistan. The news of his passing struck me deeply, leaving a profound sense of loss and sadness. Reflecting on his guidance and impact on my climbing journey, I couldn't help but feel a mix of emotions— gratitude for his inspiration, regret for not having the opportunity to express my appreciation, and a profound realization of the impermanence of life.

Mario's influence on my climbing pursuits was immeasurable. He was more than a guide; he was a source of support and motivation during moments of exhaustion and doubt. I vividly recalled those instances when, fatigued and on the verge of giving up, his words of encouragement spurred me onward. His belief in my abilities ignited a spark within me, propelling me to persevere and overcome challenges that seemed insurmountable.

Though I never had the opportunity to directly thank Mario, his spirit lived on in my continued pursuits, in the challenges I overcame, and in the heights I reached. His memory spurred me to pay forward his inspiration, becoming a source of encouragement for others seeking to conquer their own summits. And as I faced new mountains, both literal and metaphorical, I carried with me the lessons he had imparted—lessons of resilience, determination, and the enduring power of human connection.

Climbing Aconcagua prior to the earthquake was a significant milestone that ignited a surge of confidence within me. The triumph of conquering its heights served as a stepping stone towards my audacious goal of scaling Everest in 2015.

However, the landscape of my journey shifted dramatically after the earthquake in 2015. The subsequent climbs of the remaining 7 summits were marked by a different context, one shaped by the aftermath of the earthquake. The resilience of the mountains I climbed mirrored the resilience I witnessed in the communities affected by the earthquake. The challenges and triumphs I experienced on these post-earthquake ascents took on a new layer of meaning, reflecting both personal growth and a shared journey of recovery.

Chapter 8

2nd Summit: Kilimanjaro

Out of the 7 summits Kilimanjaro is the most undemanding mountain. It was a remarkable adventure that unfolded with every step, revealing the awe-inspiring beauty and challenges of Africa's highest peak. As I embarked on this journey, I knew that Mount Kilimanjaro's diverse ecosystems and demanding terrain would test my physical and mental endurance.

The ascent of Kilimanjaro comprises several distinct routes, each offering a unique experience. I chose the Machame Route, renowned for its stunning landscapes and gradual acclimatization. The trail began through lush rainforests, with emerald foliage enveloping us as we trekked upward. The air was thick with humidity, a stark contrast to the crisp heights awaiting us.

The first camp, Machame Camp, nestled at around 9,900 feet, marked the end of our initial day's trek. The sounds of the forest enveloped us as we settled into camp, surrounded by fellow trekkers who, like me, were eager to conquer the mountain's challenges. As we prepared for the next day's climb, the excitement mingled with a hint of apprehension, knowing that the ascent would only grow steeper and more demanding.

The Shira Plateau, our next destination, beckoned with its surreal expanse at approximately 12,600 feet. The rugged terrain and barren landscapes transported us to a world unlike any other.

The thinning air was a constant reminder of the altitude's effects, as our bodies adapted to the ever-changing environment. Acclimatization hikes provided both preparation and stunning vistas, as the glaciers and peaks loomed above us, a reminder of the heights we aimed to conquer.

The journey continued through Barranco Camp, perched around 13,000 feet. The Barranco Wall, an imposing rock face, tested our climbing skills and mental fortitude. With careful footwork and the guidance of our experienced guides, we scaled the wall, each step bringing us closer to the craggy ridges that lay ahead.

Karanga Camp, at approximately 13,100 feet, greeted us with its rocky terrain and sweeping panoramas. The air grew thinner as we approached the lofty heights, but our acclimatization hikes and gradual progress minimized the impact. The camaraderie among trekkers served as a constant source of motivation, reminding us that we were all united in the pursuit of a common goal.

Approaching the summit push, Barafu Camp awaited us at about 15,200 feet. Here, we made our final preparations for the ascent to Uhuru Peak, the highest point of Kilimanjaro. The atmosphere was charged with anticipation and excitement, tempered by the realization that the summit push would test our limits in ways we had yet to experience.

The final night ascent began under a blanket of stars, with headlamps illuminating the path ahead. The air grew thinner, and each step felt like an arduous feat. The cold seeped into our bones, a stark reminder of the altitude's unforgiving grip. But with unwavering determination and the support of our guides, we persisted.

And then, as the first rays of dawn painted the sky with hues of gold and pink, we stood at the summit, Uhuru Peak, at an awe-inspiring elevation of 19,341 feet. The exhaustion and challenges of the climb melted away in the face of this extraordinary achievement. The sense of accomplishment and elation was overwhelming, as we reveled in the beauty of the landscape below and the triumph of conquering Kilimanjaro's formidable heights.

Descending to Mweka Camp, we reflected on the journey—a journey that had tested our physical and mental limits, exposed us to breathtaking vistas, and introduced us to a sense of camaraderie and determination that transcended language and culture. Kilimanjaro's diverse ecosystems, steep climbs, and high-altitude challenges had transformed us, leaving an indelible mark on our souls.

Serengeti

The conclusion of my Kilimanjaro climb marked the beginning of a different yet equally awe-inspiring adventure. After descending from the heights of Kilimanjaro, I embarked on a captivating journey through the heart of the African wilderness. The vast landscapes of Serengeti and Ngorongoro unfolded before me, offering a front-row seat to the wonders of nature.

The transition from the rugged terrain of Kilimanjaro to the expansive plains of Serengeti was a breathtaking contrast. As I ventured into the Serengeti National Park, I was greeted by a symphony of wildlife. Herds of graceful antelopes grazed alongside powerful elephants, while curious giraffes stretched their necks to reach tender leaves. Lions prowled through the golden grasses, their majestic presence a testament to the untamed beauty of the wilderness.

Ngorongoro Crater, a true natural wonder, welcomed me with its breathtaking vistas. The crater's bowl-like expanse was a sanctuary for a diverse array of animals, creating an intimate and harmonious coexistence within its confines. I watched in awe as rhinos, zebras, and wildebeests traversed the landscape, their interactions painting a vivid picture of the circle of life.

The safaris offered a unique perspective on the intricacies of nature, capturing the delicate balance that sustains life within these remarkable ecosystems. Every turn revealed a new chapter of the animal kingdom's story, each encounter leaving an indelible mark on my heart and soul.

As I observed these incredible creatures in their natural habitat, I felt a profound sense of connection to the intricate web of life that enveloped me. The safaris provided a moment of reflection, a chance to appreciate the boundless beauty of our planet and the importance of conservation efforts to protect these precious habitats.

In a sense, the safaris served as a poignant continuation of the Kilimanjaro climb—an exploration of different facets of our world's wonders. Just as the mountain's challenges had pushed my limits and expanded my horizons, the safari experience was a reminder of the vastness of our planet and the incredible diversity it harbors.

As I witnessed the dance of life on the African plains, I couldn't help but feel a deep sense of gratitude for the opportunity to be a part of these awe-inspiring moments. The combination of conquering Kilimanjaro's heights and immersing myself in the wild beauty of Serengeti and Ngorongoro created a harmonious symphony of experiences, each note contributing to the rich tapestry of my journey.

Kupona Foundation, CCBRT Center, Tanzania

One of the most meaningful and impactful moments of my journey unfolded as I ventured from Kilimanjaro to Dar es Salaam, a short hour's flight away. It was here that I had the privilege of meeting the remarkable women of the Kupona Foundation, the very organization for which I had embarked on this monumental climb—a climb that aimed to raise both funds and awareness for their important cause.

The essence of Kupona is deeply rooted in empowering individuals and communities across Tanzania to realize their full potential by improving their access to vital healthcare services. Their mission resonated with me profoundly, as I understood the transformative power that optimal health holds in breaking the cycle of poverty and fostering thriving families.

At the heart of this movement is the Comprehensive Community Based Rehabilitation in Tanzania (CCBRT), a leading healthcare provider headquartered in Dar es Salaam. CCBRT's expertise extends to disability care, making them a vital partner of the Tanzanian Government in the ongoing effort to enhance maternal and newborn healthcare. Beyond their impressive statistics of providing over 100,000 clinical consultations and conducting more than 10,000 surgical procedures annually, CCBRT is committed to sharing their knowledge and skills to strengthen healthcare systems both locally and globally.

One of the poignant focuses of Kupona Foundation is aiding women who have suffered from fistula, a devastating condition that warrants specialized treatment and care. These women, who have faced immense challenges, are offered the hope and support they deserve through Kupona's dedicated initiatives.

Meeting these resilient women and witnessing the impact of the Kupona Foundation firsthand was a profound experience that left an indelible mark on my journey. As I engaged with these individuals and learned about their stories, I was reminded of the far-reaching effects of empowerment and access to healthcare. The synergy between my climb and the Foundation's mission became evident, underscoring the interconnectedness of our global community.

The encounter with Kupona Foundation's work gave purpose and depth to my pursuit of the 7 summits. It was a reminder that our endeavors, no matter how challenging or grand, can be channeled into tangible change and the betterment of lives. As I reflected on this intersection of personal ambition and collective impact, I was filled with a profound sense of fulfillment and determination to continue championing these vital causes.

Chapter 9

3rd Summit: Elbrus

Climbing Mount Elbrus was an expedition that beckoned with both anticipation and a hint of trepidation. As I stood at the base of Europe's highest peak, the towering majesty of Elbrus seemed to reach out, both daunting and exhilarating. This was a new chapter in my journey towards conquering the 7 summits, and I was ready to embrace the challenges that lay ahead.

The journey began at the lower camps, each step carrying me closer to the summit. The Base Camp, nestled amidst a stunning landscape, served as our starting point. It was a place where climbers from around the world converged, a vibrant tapestry of shared aspirations and camaraderie. Here, I embarked on a gradual ascent, the surrounding beauty serving as a constant reminder of the reward that awaited at the peak.

Progressing to higher camps, the terrain grew more demanding. The Intermediate Camp presented a breathtaking vista, a surreal juxtaposition of stark wilderness against the backdrop of distant horizons. The thinning air was a reminder of the altitude's unyielding grip, a challenge that both my body and mind had to contend with.

Acclimatization was paramount as I moved to the Pastukhov Rocks, navigating through rocky passages and snow-covered expanses. Every step was a testament to endurance, a dance with the elements that both humbled and invigorated. And as I advanced further, I felt the weight of each footfall, a physical manifestation of the altitude's unforgiving embrace.

The final stretch to the summit loomed, a culmination of perseverance and determination. The saddle between Elbrus's twin peaks marked a pivotal juncture, a place where the winds whispered tales of triumph and resilience. The ascent to the West Summit was a formidable challenge, a steep ascent where ice and snow became both allies and adversaries.

As I neared the summit, my heart surged with a mix of emotions—awe, exhilaration, and a deep-seated pride. The view from the peak was nothing short of spectacular, an unobstructed panorama that stretched across vast landscapes. I felt a profound sense of accomplishment, as though the challenges of the journey had converged into this singular moment of triumph.

But even as I celebrated this personal victory, I was reminded of the collective effort that had propelled me to this pinnacle. The camaraderie of fellow climbers, the guidance of experienced guides—it was a tapestry woven by many hands, a reminder of the interconnectedness of our shared pursuit.

Descending from Elbrus, the journey's end was met with a mix of emotions. The mountain had tested my limits, pushing me beyond what I thought possible. It had taught me the value of resilience, the importance of preparation, and the beauty of surrendering to nature's grandeur.

Mount Elbrus stood not only as a physical conquest, but as a chapter etched with stories of courage, persistence, and a deep appreciation for the world's untamed beauty. It was a testament to the power of the human spirit, a reflection of our capacity to reach new heights—both within ourselves and atop the summits we dare to ascend.

Climbing Mount Elbrus immersed me not only in the rugged grandeur of the Caucasus Range but also in the unique world of local Russian climbers. Their profound connection to the mountains was evident in their approach, an embodiment of reverence and seriousness that resonated deeply with me. As I mingled with these climbers, I gained insights into their unwavering dedication and the cultural tapestry that enriched their alpine pursuits.

The local Russian climbers exhibited a level of discipline and preparation that mirrored the imposing nature of Elbrus itself. Their meticulous attention to gear and techniques spoke volumes about their commitment to their craft. Every interaction was steeped in a shared understanding of the mountains' unpredictable temperament and the necessity for preparedness. Conversations were punctuated with stories of legendary ascents and near-misses, underscoring the gravity of their chosen path.

Their camaraderie was tangible, a unity forged through shared challenges and triumphs. It was a privilege to be welcomed into their fold, to glean from their experiences and insights. The language of climbing proved universal, transcending linguistic barriers as we traded tales of other peaks and exchanged hard-earned wisdom.

Beyond the exhilaration of the climb, a vibrant cultural experience awaited me in St. Petersburg. The city's rich history and artistic splendor beckoned, offering a compelling counterpoint to the rugged landscapes I had grown accustomed to. Wandering through the storied streets, I was enveloped by the grandeur of architectural masterpieces, each facade a testament to the city's rich heritage.

The Hermitage Museum, a treasure trove of artistic brilliance, drew me into a world of masterful brushstrokes and timeless sculptures. The echoes of history reverberated within the walls of the Winter Palace, each room a tableau of opulence and opulent tales. It was a stark departure from the raw wilderness of Elbrus, an immersion in the cultural tapestry of a nation known for its artistic prowess.

As I wandered along the banks of the Neva River, I marveled at the blend of tradition and modernity that characterized St. Petersburg. The city's vibrant energy was palpable, an embodiment of the diverse facets that make Russia a tapestry of contrasts. From the regal palaces to the bustling markets, each corner unveiled a new layer of the city's essence.

The juxtaposition of my climbing journey with the cultural exploration in St. Petersburg created a harmonious symphony of experiences. It was a reminder that adventure, in all its forms, weaves a narrative that enriches our lives. Whether ascending the heights of Elbrus or immersing oneself in the artistic wonders of a city, every step is a testament to our boundless curiosity and the human spirit's thirst for exploration.

In the end, my time in Russia was not just about reaching summits or exploring cities; it was about forging connections—with nature, with fellow climbers, and with the tapestry of cultures that paint our world in vibrant hues. It was a reminder that every climb, every journey, is a step towards embracing the world in all its beauty and complexity.

Chapter 10

4th Summit: Vinson Massif

Climbing Vinson Massif was an extraordinary expedition that transported me to the mesmerizing landscapes of Antarctica. The sheer remoteness and otherworldly beauty of this icy continent held an allure that was both humbling and exhilarating. As I embarked on this leg of my journey towards conquering the 7 summits, I found myself immersed in a realm that seemed to exist beyond time and space.

Our journey began with a flight to Punta Arenas, Chile, a gateway to the frozen expanse of Antarctica. The anticipation was palpable as we soared over vast oceans, the promise of adventure glinting on the horizon. Aboard the Russian Ilyushin Il-76, I marveled at the enormity of this flying fortress, a testament to human ingenuity in the face of Earth's most extreme environments.

Landing on the pristine expanse of Union Glacier, the sheer magnitude of Antarctica's untouched beauty washed over me. The virginal landscapes stretched as far as the eye could see, an uninterrupted canvas of white punctuated by craggy peaks. It was a realm of silence, where nature reigned supreme, and our presence felt like a fleeting whisper against the eternal expanse.

The base camp on Union Glacier hummed with activity, a microcosm of diverse individuals united by a common goal—the pursuit of exploration and discovery. Here, scientists from around the world converged, bringing with them a kaleidoscope of knowledge and insights. Conversations were a symphony of languages and perspectives, a celebration of our shared curiosity about the world's most enigmatic continent.

Our journey to Vinson Massif began with treks through the icy terrain, each step a dance with the elements. The camps were vital oases, temporary shelters against the frigid embrace of Antarctica's cold embrace. From Base Camp to Camp 1, the landscape shifted with every stride, revealing glaciers and seracs that whispered stories of eons past.

As I ascended higher, the challenges intensified. The higher camps demanded more than physical endurance; they called for a profound mental fortitude. The thin air left its mark, a constant reminder of the altitude's grasp on my being. It was a dance of pacing and perseverance, where every breath held the promise of bringing me closer to the summit.

The summit push was a culmination of all that had come before— a testament to preparation, resilience, and determination. As I stood atop Vinson Massif, the view was a panorama of unadulterated splendor. Antarctica's icy majesty stretched to the horizon, a vista that transcended words. It was a reminder of nature's grandeur, a humbling realization of our place within its intricate tapestry.

The descent was a journey of reflection and gratitude, each step retracing the path I had forged to the summit. Back at Union Glacier, conversations flowed like tributaries converging into a river of shared experiences. The sense of unity and camaraderie was undeniable, a reminder that our quests—whether scientific or alpine—were threads woven into the fabric of Antarctica's story.

High Camp, Banner of Omid Foundation

Climbing Vinson Massif held a deeper purpose beyond personal achievement like all the other 7 summits —it was a call to raise awareness and support for those who have suffered abuse and violence in Iran and Afghanistan. As I embarked on this monumental ascent, the mountain became a symbol of resilience and hope, a platform to amplify the voices of those who have endured hardships.

At 16,000 feet, the altitude mirrored the uphill battle that survivors of abuse face each day. With determination, I pledged to raise $16,000 for the Omid Foundation, an organization that provided a lifeline to those in need. Their mission was to empower and uplift individuals who had faced unimaginable challenges, offering a beacon of light amidst the shadows.

The climb became a poignant metaphor for the journey of healing and transformation that survivors undertake. Just as I navigated treacherous terrain, battling icy slopes and biting winds, these survivors confronted their own internal struggles and external obstacles. The parallels were striking—the climb was a tangible manifestation of the resilience that defines the human spirit.

With each step I took towards the summit, I carried the stories and hopes of those whose lives had been scarred by abuse. The weight of their experiences fueled my determination, propelling me forward even when the path seemed insurmountable. As the altitude increased, so did my commitment to making a difference, to being a voice for the voiceless.

Upon reaching the pinnacle of Vinson Massif, the victory was shared not only by me but by the countless individuals who had supported this cause. The view from the top was not just a breathtaking vista of Antarctica's splendor; it was a glimpse into a world where compassion and solidarity triumph over adversity. It was a moment of triumph, a celebration of the resilience that unites survivors and climbers alike.

As I descended from the summit, the echoes of my footsteps reverberated with the purpose that had driven me to undertake this journey. The funds raised, a testament to the collective effort, would serve as a lifeline for those seeking solace and empowerment. And though the mountain's icy embrace gave way to the warmth of home, the memories of this climb would forever remind me of the power of unity and the strength that lies within us all.

Storm

During my ascen, Mother Nature unleashed her fury in the form of a colossal storm. Roaring winds at a staggering 80 mph swept across the terrain, shattering the tranquility that had enveloped us. Our sturdy tents, usually our refuge, were no match for this tempest, and the gusts tore through them with unrelenting force.

In the midst of this chaos, a sense of unity emerged among our team. Huddled together in my tent, my fellow climbers sought shelter from the relentless onslaught. It was a moment of camaraderie that transcended gender boundaries—I, the sole female climber, stood side by side with my male teammates, facing nature's wrath together.

As the storm raged outside, our world within the tent became a sanctuary, albeit a cramped one. The howling winds and the violent shaking of the tent trapped us inside, rendering us immobile. The passage of time seemed distorted, and a surreal stillness settled over us. For an agonizing 24 hours, we were ensnared in this canvas cocoon, unable to venture out and face the elements.

Surviving in these confined quarters without sustenance became our challenge. Food and water became inaccessible, a reminder of our vulnerability in the face of nature's fury. However, a silver lining emerged amidst the adversity—my stash of chocolate, carefully packed for the journey, became a beacon of comfort. In the midst of uncertainty, these sweet morsels became a source of solace, offering a momentary respite from the turmoil outside.

As I shared my precious chocolate with my fellow climbers, a bond of gratitude and resilience deepened. In this dire situation, our reliance on each other grew stronger. Conversations ebbed and flowed, stories were shared, and amidst the chaos, laughter occasionally punctuated the air. It was a reminder of the human spirit's ability to find light even in the darkest of circumstances.

Eventually, the storm's fury began to subside, and the wind's relentless howl transformed into a mere whisper. The tent, battered and bruised, stood as a testament to our endurance. When we finally emerged from our makeshift shelter, the landscape that greeted us bore the marks of the tempest's wrath—yet we emerged unbroken, a testament to our shared strength and resilience.

In retrospect, that harrowing experience became a defining chapter of our journey. The storm underscored the unpredictable nature of mountain climbing and the unwavering bond that forms among climbers in the face of adversity. And while the winds may have shattered our tents, they couldn't extinguish the flame of camaraderie that burned brightly within our hearts.

Chapter 11

Greenland

The awe-inspiring beauty of Antarctica left an indelible mark on my spirit, igniting a spark of inspiration that would soon drive me to embark on a new and audacious adventure. As I mingled with athletes who had conquered the unforgiving terrain and crossed the icy expanse to reach the South Pole, a newfound determination began to take root within me. Their stories of triumph over the frozen wilderness resonated deeply, and I found myself yearning to test my limits once again.

The allure of crossing Greenland, an untamed land of ice, beckoned to me with its siren call. The images of majestic glaciers, towering ice formations, and the sheer thrill of conquering such a formidable challenge danced before my mind's eye. It was as if Antarctica had awakened a dormant spirit within me, a spirit that hungered for the thrill of adventure and the taste of the unknown.

Embarking on the journey of crossing Greenland from west to east was a true test of endurance, resilience, and the sheer bounds of human determination. As I strapped on my skis for the next 350 miles and harnessed the weight of two sleds, each laden with a staggering load of 60 pounds, I knew that the next 30 days would be a relentless dance between exertion and awe-inspiring beauty.

Greenland, a vast expanse of ice and snow, welcomed me with an otherworldly panorama. The landscape stretched out in all directions, a sea of white punctuated only by the contours of the ice beneath my feet. It was as if I had stepped into a vast ping pong ball, where the world was rendered in shades of white and gray, and the overcast sky melded seamlessly with the frozen ground. The strong winds whispered tales of the land's untamed spirit, a constant companion as I forged ahead.

The weight of my sleds bore down on me, a reminder of the colossal challenge that lay before me. With each step, the skis glided over the icy terrain, and the rhythmic swish of the skis provided a soothing cadence amidst the solitude. The journey was marked by a relentless push forward, a delicate balance between conserving energy and conquering distance.

The true beauty of this frozen world, however, revealed itself during the quiet moments. As the sun dipped below the horizon, painting the sky with hues of orange and pink, the stage was set for the most enchanting spectacle—the Northern lights. Dancing across the night sky in ethereal waves of green and purple, the lights seemed to tell stories of a world beyond the ordinary, a realm of magic and wonder that existed far beyond the icy plains.

Amidst this stark beauty, there were also poignant reminders of human presence. Passing by the remnants of the Distant Early Warning Line sites, once manned by brave souls who stood guard against potential threats, I couldn't help but reflect on the passage of time. These structures, now abandoned and weathered, held the echoes of stories and sacrifices made in the name of vigilance.

Each day brought new challenges, from navigating crevasses to battling blizzards that seemed to engulf the world. The sleds, my steadfast companions, became a symbol of determination and perseverance. Straining against their weight, I pushed forward, etching my path across this frozen tapestry.

And then, after 30 days that felt like a lifetime of endurance and discovery, I stood at the eastern edge of Greenland, a place where the ice met the open sea. The journey had transformed me— physically, mentally, and spiritually. It was a testament to the strength that resides within, a celebration of the indomitable human spirit that drives us to conquer the impossible.

Pulling 2 Sleds Across the Greenland Glacier

The DEW Line sites, a network of radar installations established during the Cold War, were an indication to the global tensions and political complexities that defined that era. Positioned across the Arctic region, including Greenland, these sites were designed to provide early warning of potential airborne threats, particularly those originating from the Soviet Union. The sites were a symbol of defense and preparedness, a line of defense against a looming and uncertain future.

As I glided across the frozen landscapes of Greenland, I couldn't help but ponder the sudden abandonment of these once-vital installations. The silence that now enveloped these sites spoke volumes about the passage of time and the shifting tides of history. What was once a bastion of vigilance had faded into obscurity, a relic of a world no longer defined by the same geopolitical tensions.

The abruptness of the DEW Line sites' abandonment mirrored the rapid changes that often characterize the unfolding of history. As political dynamics shifted and global priorities evolved, the need for these outposts waned, leading to their eventual disuse and abandonment. The echoes of their purpose, however, lingered in the wind, a reminder of the complex interplay between nations and the inexorable march of progress.

In a curious twist of fate, the acquisition of Greenland by Denmark also cast a fascinating light on the region's history. As Denmark purchased Greenland from Norway in 1814, the icy expanse became a part of the Danish realm. This acquisition, driven by economic and strategic considerations, would shape Greenland's trajectory and relationship with the rest of the world.

As I traversed the frozen landscapes, I was amazed by the intricate history that had become an integral part of Greenland's essence. The remnants of the DEW Line sites stood as silent witnesses to a time of heightened tensions and global uncertainties, while the Danish presence underscored the intricate web of colonial legacies and territorial shifts.

Each step I took across Greenland was a tribute to the land's resilience and its ability to endure the ebb and flow of history. The whispers of the past, embodied by the DEW Line sites and the broader historical context, added a layer of depth to my journey. They reminded me that the world is full of interesting stories, each thread contributing to the rich mosaic of human experience.

Planned Parenthood

Embarking on the challenging adventure of crossing Greenland held a purpose that extended beyond the icy landscapes and freezing winds. With every stride I took across the vast expanse, I was driven by a powerful mission: to raise $10,000 for Planned Parenthood, an organization dedicated to empowering women and championing their rights.

As I navigated the unforgiving terrain, I carried with me the collective hopes and aspirations of those who believe in the importance of women's health and autonomy. Planned Parenthood's mission resonated deeply with me, and I was determined to use my journey across Greenland as a platform to raise awareness and support for their crucial work.

The organization's commitment to providing accessible healthcare, education, and resources to women across the globe spoke volumes about the transformative impact of empowering women. In a world where gender equality remains an ongoing struggle, Planned Parenthood stood as a beacon of hope, offering a lifeline of support to those who need it most.

The significance of my endeavor grew with each arduous step. Every gust of icy wind seemed to carry the voices of those who had been touched by Planned Parenthood's services, reminding me of the importance of our collective efforts. As I pushed through the challenges of hauling heavy loads and navigating treacherous terrain, I held onto the knowledge that my journey was contributing to a cause greater than myself.

As I gazed out across the vast expanse of white, I was reminded of the broader context in which my journey was unfolding. Just as Greenland's landscapes held stories of resilience and endurance, my expedition was interwoven with the narratives of countless women whose lives had been touched by the services and advocacy of Planned Parenthood.

Crossing Greenland was more than just a physical feat; it was a symbolic gesture of solidarity and support for women everywhere. With every step I took, I was carrying the hopes of those who believe in the importance of empowering women and ensuring their right to health and autonomy. The beauty of the icy landscapes mirrored the beauty of the cause, both indicates the strength and resilience of the human spirit. And so, as I navigated the frozen wilderness, I knew that my journey was part of a much larger narrative—one of empowerment, equality, and the pursuit of a brighter future for all.

Chapter 12

5th Climb Carstenz Pyramids

Embarking on the journey to conquer Carstensz Pyramid in Indonesia was a whirlwind of unexpected trials and eye-opening insights. As I landed on Indonesian soil, the allure of a new adventure beckoned, though little did I fathom the tumultuous path that lay ahead.

Upon arrival at the mountain's base camp, a cocktail of excitement and uncertainty coursed through my veins. I readied my gear, eager to tackle the upcoming climb. However, nature had other plans, casting us into a relentless cycle of rain that transformed our base camp into a watery refuge. Ten days passed as the rain poured relentlessly from the sky, ensnaring us in a damp cocoon.

At an elevation of 16,024 feet (4,884 meters), Carstensz Pyramid commanded both awe and trepidation. Our ascent was further complicated by the precarious element of traversing ropes to conquer its summit. The mountain itself posed dangers aplenty, with rugged terrain and vertiginous slopes that challenged our every step. But the most daunting facet was the need to tread through a labyrinthine web of villages, each inhabited by distinct tribes. While their vibrant cultures fascinated, we knew to approach them with respect and caution, aware of potential pitfalls amidst the intrigue.

Yet another enigma loomed—the presence of a gold mine nestled in the mountain's vicinity. The discord between economic interests and ecological preservation echoed through the community, casting a shadow over our climb. The ethical quagmire of profiting against the backdrop of environmental concerns underscored the complexity of the region's challenges.

As the rain finally relented, the moment to ascend arrived. Each step towards the summit seemed to hold the weight of every challenge we had faced. The culmination of our efforts was heightened by the precarious rope walk—a vertical traverse that defied gravity itself. The danger was palpable, amplifying the thrill of our ascent.

Standing at the apex, 16,024 feet above the earth, the vista before me was an exquisite blend of triumph and humility. I marveled at the panorama while pondering the tumultuous journey that led me here—the rain-soaked base camp, the cultural nuances, the ethical dilemmas, the ropes that had bridged the gap between land and sky.

In conquering Carstensz Pyramid, I hadn't merely surmounted a mountain; I had explored the intricate layers of a region's history, culture, and environmental dynamics. As I surveyed the expanse from the summit, I recognized that this climb had evolved into a profound narrative of resilience, connection, and the intricate dance between mankind and nature.

Building a Portable Tent School for Syrian Refugees

The decision to embark on the challenging ascent of Carstensz Pyramid was deeply rooted in a profound sense of purpose. It was a purpose that went beyond personal achievement, extending its reach to those whose lives had been shattered by the horrors of conflict and displacement. The catalyst for this dedication was a heart-wrenching revelation – the news of Syrian families desperately attempting to escape their war-torn homeland, tragically perishing at sea as they sought refuge in Europe.

The weight of this heartbreaking reality pressed upon me, fueling an unwavering determination to make a difference. It was the women among the Syrian refugees who occupied the forefront of my thoughts. In times of war and disaster, they bear a disproportionate burden of suffering, often finding themselves in the gravest danger. Their resilience and tenacity in the face of adversity inspired me deeply, and I knew that I had to take action.

The mountain, became a symbol of both the daunting challenges faced by refugees and the heights of hope that they aspire to reach. Every step I took up those rugged slopes was imbued with the stories of the brave Syrian women who navigate unimaginable hardships with unwavering strength.

The very ropes that I clung to during precarious climbs mirrored the tightropes of survival that these women tread upon daily. Their journeys are often filled with uncertainty, danger, and the need to navigate treacherous paths for the sake of their families' safety.

As I battled against the elements and pushed my limits on Carstensz Pyramid, I channeled the courage and resilience of these women. I climbed not only for myself but also to amplify the voices of those who have been silenced by conflict and displacement. The climb was a testament to their endurance, a dedication to their struggle, and a call to action for a world that must stand in solidarity with their plight.

Standing atop the summit, I felt a profound connection with the resilience of the Syrian refugee women. Their journeys are marked by hardships and loss, yet they persist with incredible strength, seeking safety and a better future. The climb was a tribute to their spirit, a declaration that their struggles would not go unnoticed, and a commitment to amplifying their stories.

This climb was a resounding reminder that the challenges faced by refugee women are shared challenges that demand collective action. Their strength and resilience serve as a beacon of hope, motivating us to continue raising awareness, advocating for change, and offering support to those who need it most. With every step I took, I carried the stories of these women with me, and as I descended from the summit, their spirit remained a driving force to create a better world for them and all who are affected by conflict and displacement.

Divorced

In the context of this climb, my therapist cautioned that I might not be ready. She advised me to stay home and cancel the expedition, considering the recent divorce and the potential risks associated with my emotional state. Despite her concerns, I chose to press on, determined to conquer the mountain and driven by helping the Syrian refugees. And I did succeed in reaching the summit, proving to myself that I could overcome challenges even in the face of adversity.

However, it was during the ten days of being confined to our tents due to relentless rain that I found an unexpected source of solace. I turned to an audio book that delved into the intricate process of grieving the loss of a loved one. I listened to this book not just once, but ten times over. It felt like a divine gift, a way for me to navigate and process the aftermath of my divorce.

As rain drummed relentlessly on the tent, I allowed the wisdom from the book to seep into my thoughts. Each repetition helped me unravel the tangles of emotion, allowing me to confront the pain, accept the changes, and begin the healing journey. Those ten times became a profound gift from the universe, guiding me through the intricate terrain of my emotions and providing me with a valuable tool to process the complexities of my divorce.

Chapter 13

6th Climb: Denali

As the highest peak in North America, towering at an elevation of 20,310 feet, it held a special place on my journey to conquer the Seven Summits. But Denali wasn't just a mountain; it was a fierce and formidable force of nature that demanded the utmost respect.

My adventure began with a flight to the base camp in the heart of breathtaking Alaska. The surrounding landscape was a portrait of rugged beauty, with vast glaciers and snow-covered expanses stretching out before me. The air held a tangible sense of excitement and anticipation, knowing that this climb would test me in ways I had never experienced before.

The camps on Denali were strategic refuges that offered both respite and challenges. Each one marked a significant milestone on the path to the summit. From the initial base camp to the higher camps that became stepping stones toward the pinnacle, they provided a sense of progress and accomplishment amid the harsh environment.

But Denali was not to be underestimated. It demanded rigorous preparation. Training involved carrying a backpack weighing 85 pounds, nearly equivalent to my own body weight of 120 pounds. At times, the weight felt crushing, and I stumbled under its heaviness. I vividly recall those moments in the gym when I would falter, my heavy pack threatening to topple me. Fellow gym-goers would rush to my aid, helping me rise and continue, their support a testament to the community that surrounded me.

And then came the climb itself, a true test of endurance and determination. The weather was unpredictable, and the ascent was marked by treacherous crevasses and icy slopes.

Denali was, without a doubt, the most challenging of the Seven Summits. It pushed me to my limits, both physically and mentally. But with each painstaking step, I drew strength from the stunning surroundings and the knowledge that I was conquering not only a mountain, but also my own doubts and limitations.

National Crittenton

This climb held a profound significance as it was dedicated to raising funds for the National Crittenton organization. Established in 1883, this advocacy group is acutely aware of the challenges faced by cis and trans girls, young women, and gender-expansive young individuals, especially those of color. These resilient voices often remain unheard and overlooked, lacking the attention and support they deserve in our society.

National Crittenton is a champion for those whose needs and potential have been undervalued for far too long. Their mission is fueled by the urgency to address the barriers that hinder the progress of these individuals, amplifying their voices and advocating for justice. Their work is driven by both a lack of recognition of their unique struggles and a lack of data that accurately reflects their experiences and exclusions.

In our country, there exists a concerning trend of passive and active resistance when it comes to investing in and supporting these girls, young women, and gender-expansive individuals. The absence of inclusive conversations and efforts focusing on both race/ethnicity and gender justice perpetuates this cycle of neglect. It's imperative that we recognize the intersectionality of their identities and experiences and center them in our collective pursuit of social change.

As I journeyed up the challenging slopes of Denali, I carried the stories and aspirations of these often marginalized voices with me. With every step, I was reminded of the importance of pushing boundaries not only in the physical realm but also in the realm of social justice.

My climb for National Crittenton was a symbolic ascent toward equality, representation, and empowerment. It was a way to bring attention to the urgent need for change and to shed light on the barriers that stand in the way of these girls and young women. As I stood on the summit, I knew that my journey was more than a physical feat—it was a declaration of solidarity and a commitment to breaking down the barriers that prevent these voices from being heard and valued.

Chapter 14

Last Summit

Facing the decision to return to Everest after the earthquake and avalanche was one of the most challenging moments of my life. Doubts and fears clouded my mind, and I found myself grappling with a barrage of excuses to avoid stepping back onto those formidable slopes. What if my survival in 2015 was a twist of fate, a narrow escape from a destiny that awaited me? The haunting idea that perhaps destiny had other plans lingered in my thoughts.

Yet, amidst the cacophony of doubts, there was an unbreakable promise that anchored me—a promise to my girls, a pledge that transcended fear and uncertainty. It was a promise that echoed with the voices of those who looked up to me, who found inspiration in my journey, and who held onto the belief that I could overcome any obstacle.

In the face of adversity, I realized that my journey was not just about conquering physical summits but also about conquering the limits I placed upon myself. I knew that I couldn't let fear dictate my choices and that I had to honor the promise I made to those who believed in me.

Climb Your Everest nonprofit

After dedicating eight years of my life to collaborating with various non-profit organizations dedicated to empowering women, a profound realization struck me—I was ready to embark on a new chapter by establishing my very own initiative. This decision was rooted in a multitude of factors, most notably my extensive background in women's empowerment and the culmination of my PhD research dissertation on this pivotal subject.

Having worked alongside different organizations, including my continued involvement with ENG (Empower Nepali Girls), I felt an innate calling to expand my reach beyond borders. The plight of women in Afghanistan, where circumstances are undeniably harsh and extreme, resonated deeply with me. It was within this challenging environment that I saw an opportunity to channel my efforts towards a broader mission.

Thus, fueled by a burning desire to amplify my impact and driven by the insights gained through my academic pursuits, I took a monumental step forward. I founded my very own non-profit, a venture that was both a culmination of years of dedication and a fresh beginning. This new endeavor was a testament to my unwavering commitment to empower women globally, utilizing not only the knowledge I had amassed but also the passion that ignited within me.

As I embarked on this journey, my vision extended far and wide, encompassing nations and cultures far removed from my own. Afghanistan, standing as a symbol of adversity and resilience, held a special place in my heart. I was resolved to bring change to the lives of women who faced unparalleled challenges in their daily existence.

In a tearful fusion of purpose and determination, I made a profound decision—to dedicate my upcoming Everest climb to raising funds for my newly established non-profit CYE. The towering peak of Everest stood as a poignant metaphor for the challenges faced by the women I sought to empower.

Every step I took on that treacherous ascent was a testament to the indomitable spirit of women, a reminder that challenges could be overcome, and dreams could be achieved.

Training for Everest

In the quest to prepare for my second ascent of Everest, the endeavor was undeniably more demanding. This time around, I faced the reality of being 41 years old, acutely aware that my body's ability to recover had evolved since my earlier climbs. This awareness brought forth a new dimension to my training—a recognition that I needed to push myself even harder to achieve the pinnacle of physical and mental preparedness.

So, I made a pivotal decision to enlist the guidance of a seasoned coach named Tim. Renowned for his expertise in preparing elite athletes and mountaineers, Tim introduced me to a surprising revelation that would fundamentally reshape my approach. He emphasized that our focus would extend far beyond the realm of physical strength and endurance—it was the landscape of my mind that we would traverse extensively. Tim's promise was bold: he intended to push me to a realm beyond my perceived limits, a space where uncertainty reigned and self-discovery flourished. This transformation wasn't confined to the mountain; it was designed to enrich every facet of my existence.

In the early days of our training, Tim unveiled a unique challenge that would leave a lasting mark on my memory. With an infectious grin, he gestured towards a curious contraption that bore an uncanny resemblance to a medieval relic—an apparatus adorned with weights and long ropes, poised to test my limits. This contraption, I was informed, would become my constant companion, a formidable tool in reshaping my strength and tenacity.

With Tim's voice urging me on, I embraced the challenge head-on, grappling with the discomfort and wrestling with my own limitations. It was in these moments of excruciating exertion that I discovered a surprising revelation—my ability to endure, to persevere, was rooted not merely in the physical realm but was an inseparable union of mind and body. The power of my thoughts became palpable as I navigated the treacherous path set before me.

The path wasn't without its moments of solace. Amidst the relentless training, I often found myself transported back to vivid memories of Nepal, where the laughter of scholarship girls and the rhythm of dance formed a symphony of joy. The weight of the sled would momentarily fade, replaced by the warmth of those shared moments, as if the past had woven itself into the fabric of my training.

As Tim's voice pulled me back to the present, I acknowledged the importance of embracing the pain and discomfort, of channeling my focus into each movement and breath. It was this very dedication that separated the extraordinary from the ordinary, the great from the good. And in each stride, each pull of the sled, I discovered an unexpected wellspring of strength—a reservoir I knew would carry me not only up the mountains but through the vast expanse of my own potential.

On my Way to LAX Airport

The weight of anticipation hung heavy in the air as I stood before the towering heap of three massive duffel bags, each one a repository of essential gear for my upcoming 60-day Everest climb. With a mixture of excitement and trepidation, I surveyed the meticulously packed contents, a veritable arsenal designed to equip me for the formidable challenges that lay ahead.

From the outset, meticulous planning had been the linchpin of my preparations. Every item, carefully selected and methodically packed, was a lifeline—a link between the comforts of familiarity and the uncharted territory of the world's highest peak. I ran through a mental checklist, my mind flipping through the countless details I had scrutinized, revised, and perfected.

Harnesses, carabiners, ropes—my fingers traced over the metallic essentials that would tether me to the mountain's icy embrace. Layers of insulated clothing, meticulously chosen to ward off the unforgiving cold, lay stacked with precision. High-tech gear vied for space with tried-and-true tools, each item serving a specific purpose in the intricate puzzle that was my climb.

Yet, despite the meticulous preparations, a nagging whisper of doubt lingered in my mind. What if something crucial had slipped through the cracks?

As I contemplated this question, a heartwarming chorus of voices resonated in the distance, drawing my attention beyond the jumble of gear. Turning towards the source, I was met with a scene that felt like a warm embrace—the faces of friends and family had gathered, their presence a testament to the unwavering support that had propelled me thus far.

Their smiles, their words of encouragement, their reassuring gestures—these were the emotional ballast that steadied me against the tempestuous sea of doubts. Their presence transformed the sterile airport terminal into a sanctuary of camaraderie and shared aspirations.

As I embraced my loved ones, gratitude welled within me, mingling with the hum of excitement that pulsed through my veins. I looked around at the faces, each one a reflection of the myriad reasons behind my quest. Their words, laden with good wishes and blessings, carried with them the hopes and dreams of not just me, but an entire community that had rallied behind this endeavor.

Lukla Airport

Tenzing-Hillary Airport, commonly known as Lukla Airport in Nepal, serves as a crucial gateway for trekkers and climbers embarking on the journey to Mount Everest. This remote Himalayan settlement, perched at an elevation of 9,383 feet above sea level, holds the promise of adventure and breathtaking vistas, but it also harbors a unique set of challenges and risks that travelers must confront even before they set foot on the mountain.

Lukla serves as the point of entry for all Everest climbers, offering a relatively faster alternative to days of arduous trekking through rugged terrain. The preferred mode of transport is a short flight that shuttles hikers between Kathmandu and Lukla multiple times a day. While the flight duration is a mere 25-30 minutes, the experience at these two airports could not be more disparate.

Lukla Airport stands as a stark testament to the inherent difficulties that come with operating in high-altitude and mountainous regions. The very nature of these conditions poses formidable challenges to pilots as they navigate their aircraft into and out of this diminutive airfield. The thin air at high altitudes reduces air pressure, impacting the aircraft's handling and performance. This atmospheric quirk requires pilots to exhibit exceptional skill and precision during takeoffs and landings, with little margin for error.

The runway at Lukla is notably short, adding an extra layer of complexity to the pilot's task. The geography surrounding the airport further amplifies the risks, as towering mountains envelop the airstrip, leaving minimal room for maneuvering. Wind shear, a phenomenon where sudden changes in wind speed and direction occur, can pose a significant threat, further challenging pilots' capabilities.

Namche Bazzar

After a couple of days of trekking along the scenic trail, we finally reached Namche Bazaar. This bustling village, surprisingly sizable for such a remote region, serves as a vital hub for both climbers and trekkers en route to Base Camp. Its role extends beyond the mountain enthusiasts, as local residents also gather here for the weekly markets, creating a vibrant and diverse atmosphere.

Namche Bazaar offers a range of amenities that cater to the needs of those embarking on mountain journeys. Amidst the stunning backdrop of the surrounding peaks, you'll find shops stocked not only with climbing equipment and supplies, but also charming bakeries and tourist boutiques. The village, perched on the slope, seems to blend seamlessly with the natural beauty of the Himalayan landscape.

Our trek led us through the valley and up a steep ascent to the lodge where we would be lodging for the night. I found myself walking alongside Joe, a European companion whose inquisitive nature led us into engaging conversations. He was particularly interested in my insights on encouraging girls and women to pursue engineering—a challenge that resonated not only in Nepal but also in my own experiences back home. The scarcity of women in technical fields like engineering was a common trend, and Joe and I delved into a discussion about how to foster diversity in traditionally male-dominated professions.

As we shared our thoughts, Kelly, my tentmate, joined our conversation. The dialogue naturally shifted to another intriguing topic: the complexities and considerations surrounding parenthood. The three of us exchanged perspectives on family life, career aspirations, and the various choices that shape our journeys. It was a dialogue rich in diversity, mirroring the vibrant tapestry of experiences that we encountered during our trek through this remarkable region.

TengBoche

Our journey continued from Namche Bazaar, leading us to our next destination: Tengboche. This revered site, designated as a World Heritage site, is perched atop a mountain and houses a monastery where around a hundred monks reside. The trail we traversed had its unique rhythm—descending towards the glacial river, crossings over precarious suspension bridges spanning deep gorges, leading to steep ascents that demanded our determination.

With an extra day dedicated to acclimatization and recovery, we seized the opportunity to arrange an audience with the Lama, the esteemed head monk of Tengboche Monastery. His blessings were sought to accompany us on our impending journey to Everest Base Camp, a gesture of spiritual support for the challenges ahead.

Throughout our expedition to Base Camp, the trail from one village to another was spent by meaningful interactions with fellow climbers. Our path intersected with others who shared the same aspirations, each with their own unique story and motivation. A particular encounter left me pondering. There was a fellow climber, part of a different guiding company, who confessed to having little high-altitude experience aside from a single climb in the Andes. I couldn't help but wonder about the rationale behind bringing underprepared climbers to these perilous heights. The notion of inexperienced climbers navigating the same ropes and ladders as us filled me with apprehension.

Yet, amidst the challenges of the trail, the most captivating aspect of these journeys is the remarkable individuals who undertake them. As we ascended, I found myself walking alongside Garrett, our lead guide, engaged in conversation that bridged the gap between deep breaths. Amidst the thin air at an altitude of 17,000 feet, our exchange turned to personal matters. I inquired about how he managed the strain on relationships caused by his frequent absences, a subject that was important for me now that I was single given my climbing endeavors.

Garrett's candid acknowledgment resonated with me—it was true that the strain of prolonged absences could strain relationships. Yet, he also acknowledged the importance of partners who understand the passion that drives such pursuits. However, I also sensed a turning point on the horizon, recognizing that this chapter of my life would eventually reach its conclusion after the 7th summit.

Amidst the contemplative backdrop of these Himalayan landscapes, I resolved to savor each moment more deliberately. As I looked around, the panoramic views etched themselves into my memory. The surrounding peaks, the trail we tread, the camaraderie of fellow climbers—all of it became a part of the frame that shaped my journey.

Yet, the high-altitude environment also brought its challenges. Sleep was elusive, and when it did come, it was accompanied by vivid dreams that blurred the lines between reality and illusion. One night, a particularly intense dream left me momentarily disoriented the following morning, trying to converse with my teammates in Farsi before realizing it was a mere dream-induced mirage. Upon sharing my dream with them, their response was. That they wished they could speak Farsi.

As we continued our ascent towards Lobuche, a somber memorial to fallen climbers reminded us of the inherent risks of these mountains. A brass plaque embedded in the rocks bore the inscription, "May he have accomplished his dreams." Standing in silent reverence, we paid our respects, our thoughts interwoven with both the imminent dangers and the dreams we pursued.

Khumbu Icefall

The Khumbu Icefall, both alluring and perilous, stands as Everest's most captivating yet hazardous segment. Laden with deep crevasses, it conceals the abyss below—a frozen museum, seemingly crafted by an inebriated artist. Towering ice formations defy gravity, suspended at a precarious 45-degree angle, reminiscent of an eerie ice palace.

This was my exact location when my entire world was jolted by a 7.8 magnitude earthquake. Here, in this very place, lies my deepest apprehension. It's the last spot on Earth I wish to be, yet I made a promise to the girls that I'd conquer it. For seven years, I've pondered this impending encounter with the mountain, and now, as it draws near, I feel unprepared to face it once more. The weight of this stress has taken a toll on me; illness has set in, and I'm gripped by incessant coughing that defies all attempts to quell it.

For the next week, our schedule was filled with practicing and training. This was important to test how strong we were and how skilled we had become. Our guides wanted to make sure we were ready for what lay ahead. They took us to ice walls to practice using special tools on our shoes and axes. We even practiced how to rappel down cliffs and how to cross ladders over deep gaps in the ice. We practiced these things because there was a real chance of us slipping on the icy ground or falling into a deep crack. The one thing we didn't focus on much was how to handle avalanches. In many parts of the snowy area, there wasn't really anything we could do except hope for the best.

Even though it sometimes felt like I was in a busy city with all the noise, music, and conversations, I never forgot that we were in a remote and dangerous place in nature. The wind at night was so strong that it shook our tent. I couldn't sleep and worried about what would happen if the wind carried me away.

Despite the lack of sleep and my constant headache, I had to keep my mind on our tough training routine. We spent most days in the icy area called the icefall, practicing how to stay safe and move quickly across ladders. This place was one of the most dangerous spots on Earth. It felt like a living thing, growing and changing. Cracks in the ice would suddenly appear, and tall towers of ice would fall like buildings. More people died here than anywhere else on the mountain, often due to random accidents. So, when I was in this amazing, beautiful, and dangerous place, I always felt like I was holding my breath, waiting for something bad to happen. As we moved through the icy barriers, I couldn't help but think that the mountain could swallow me up in a second—walking one moment, falling through the ice the next.

The scariest part of our practice was walking on ladders over deep cracks in the ice. Sometimes, two ladders were tied together because the gap was wide. Other times, the ladders were angled or turned upwards to cross a wall of ice. Just think about how terrifying it would be to walk on a ladder over a deep, endless hole. You wouldn't even be able to see the bottom if you dared to look down. And imagine doing all of this while wearing big, heavy boots with spikes on the soles that made loud clinking sounds with each step. On top of that, we carried heavy backpacks that made it hard to keep our balance. Sometimes, the ladder was covered in slippery ice during a blizzard, and the wind was incredibly strong.

The Wall

For the past 7 years, I've envisioned this very moment. Looking at the wall! Each time, I'd attempt to divert my thoughts from my overwhelming fear, concentrating instead on the greater experience I've gained since climbing other 6 summits. Yet, despite my efforts, picturing myself on this wall remained a formidable challenge. My mind spun countless dreams where I tumbled down the face of the ice wall, plunging into the abyss of darkness and nothingness. Whenever I fell into those crevasses within my dreams, I would awaken drenched in sweat, beset by doubt and a gripping fear.

Facing that wall again brought back memories of the earthquake and avalanche. Even though we began our climb in the dark of night, as the sun rose, I found myself staring at the very same wall that I had been on during the earthquake seven years ago. I was frozen, overcome with fear, unsure of how to move forward. I had worked on healing myself and had spoken with therapists to overcome the trauma, yet here I was, still feeling its grip on me.

As I stood there, lost in my emotions, my guide called out, urging me to continue. But I hesitated, my voice trembling, "No, this is the wall." Tears streamed down my face as fear overwhelmed me. My guide questioned my tears, asking why I was crying. Through my sobs, I managed to admit, "I'm scared."

His response surprised me, "Why give the wall so much power? Don't waste your energy. You're already dehydrated." His words struck a chord within me, a reminder that I was allowing my fear to control me.

With his words in mind, I made a deal with myself: just one step at a time. I took that first step, and then another. Slowly, I moved up the wall, tears still streaming down my face. I was in the middle of the wall now, still crying, still scared. The urge to give up tugged at me, but I couldn't break the promise I had made to myself. I was determined to finish this climb, to prove to myself that I wouldn't let fear dictate my actions.

And so, step by step, tear by tear, I continued. The wall couldn't hold me back any longer. I was stronger than I thought, and with each step, I felt a sense of empowerment growing within me. I couldn't give up; I had come too far.

Acclimatization and Rope Practice

Before reaching the summit of Everest, climbers go through 3 to 4 acclimatization rotations to help their bodies adjust to the high altitude. This means I had to climb that wall a total of 6 times. The first 5 times were done before attempting the summit, and during those climbs, I had conversations with the wall. At the beginning, these talks weren't pleasant. I blamed the wall for my trauma and even my divorce.

However, something changed after I successfully reached the summit. On my way back down the wall, a different feeling emerged. I found myself thanking the wall. I thanked it for keeping me alive during the earthquake and for providing me with the chance to raise significant funds for various nonprofit organizations. It was a transformation from blame to gratitude. I had come to terms with my trauma and embraced it. This shift in perspective was the purpose of my seventh climb – a climb that symbolized acceptance and peace.

Above Base Camp

Everest has four distinct camps, each with its own character and challenges, waiting for me to conquer. My expedition began at Base Camp, a bustling hub at an elevation of approximately 17,600 feet. Camp 1, awaited me at around 19,900 feet. After leaving the comforts of Base Camp, I journeyed higher, venturing into the heart of the mountain. The first real challenge came into view—the Khumbu Icefall. That's where the wall was. Camp 1, nestled at the foot of the icefall, was a haven for acclimatization. Amidst the ice and towering seracs, I adjusted to the altitude and prepared for the next phase of the climb.

The path led to Camp 2, perched at approximately 21,300 feet. The ascent was demanding, navigating through crevasses and seracs as I made my way above the Khumbu Icefall. Camp 2, my second home on Everest, provided a breathtaking view of the Western Cwm and the formidable Lhotse Wall. It was here that I further adapted to the thin air, strengthening my body and spirit for the challenges ahead.

Climbing higher still, I reached Camp 3 at around 23,500 feet. The Lhotse Wall loomed before me—a steep and imposing obstacle. Fixed ropes guided my ascent, and each step demanded unwavering focus. At Camp 3, situated on the rugged Lhotse Wall, I steeled myself for the ascent to come. I gazed at the South Col and Lhotse, knowing that these landmarks marked my path to the summit.

Camp 3 marks the point where we begin to share tents with fellow climbers. Up until this stage, we've had our own individual tents. While there were moments of solitude that felt quite isolating, I appreciated the privacy and the ample space where I could arrange all my gear to my liking.

Our tent was positioned on a slope, and due to my tent mate's taller stature on the higher side, he would frequently slide downward during the night. This resulted in multiple instances of waking him up, urging him to return to his own sleeping pad. Despite being cocooned inside massive -40 degree sleeping bags, his occasional intrusion onto my sleeping space was tolerable. Yet, considering the challenges of sleeping at high elevations compounded by the annoyance of oxygen deficiency, the desire for a relatively comfortable sleeping arrangement became all the more essential.

The journey didn't end at Camp 3; there is one more camp beyond, each one a stepping stone toward my ultimate goal. Camp 4, known as the South Col Camp, beckoned from its perch at around 26,000 feet.

Camp 4 greeted us with relentless winds that at times seemed capable of wresting our tent away. The cacophony of flapping fabric inside the tent was so thunderous that sleep felt nearly impossible. Amidst this tempest, my excitement soared. After a decade, I was finally standing in the death zone, a mere 8 hours from the summit. Although we had our oxygen tanks on minimal flow while sleeping, we had the freedom to remove them to chat, eat, or use a pee bottle. Yet, after just a 5-minute pause from using it, the daunting struggle became apparent. A brief stroll outside to catch a glimpse of camp 4 left me slightly lightheaded. The surroundings were surprisingly littered with trash, casting a grim view of the place. Everest's proximity seemed both tantalizingly close and distressingly distant.

As I approached this final high camp, I reflected on the incredible distance I had covered, both physically and emotionally. The summit was within sight, a tantalizing challenge that demanded my all.

On Our Way to Camp 4 with Kamdorje

Leaving Camp 4, nestled on the windswept South Col at around 26,000 feet, I embarked on the most exhilarating stretch of my journey – the final ascent to the summit of Everest. The air was thin, and every breath was a precious commodity, urging me to move efficiently and purposefully.

At 2am May 20th, 2022, as I set out from Camp 4, the imposing slopes of the Triangular Face lay before me. This section of the climb demanded both physical prowess and mental fortitude. The path wound its way through a maze of snow and ice, zigzagging its ascent. The slopes were steep and the terrain treacherous, requiring me to rely heavily on my crampons and ascender tool. The ice beneath my feet was crisp, and I took deliberate steps, my heart pounding with each movement. A trail of headlamps illuminated the ascent from camp 4 to the balcony, painting a breathtaking scene of beauty across the mountain.

Reaching the Balcony around sunrise, a relatively flat section of the climb at around 27,600 feet, provided a brief respite. I paused to catch my breath, change my oxygen tank, and take in the breathtaking panorama that surrounded me. To the south, the sweeping expanse of the Western Cwm stretched out like a vast amphitheater, while to the north, the imposing Lhotse Wall towered in all its grandeur.

Leaving the Balcony behind, I continued my ascent towards the South Summit, a crucial landmark at approximately 28,700 feet. The South Summit is a false peak that can easily deceive the untrained eye, but experienced climbers recognized it as a pivotal moment. The knife-edge ridge leading to the South Summit required focused balance and surefootedness, as the drop-offs on either side were sheer and dizzying.

As I conquered the South Summit, my gaze was drawn to the legendary Hillary Step, a steep rock wall rising up like a sentinel at about 28,840 feet. This iconic section of the climb used to be a technical challenge, however, it changed after the earthquake! The vertical ascent was a culmination of both physical and mental strength, and the sense of achievement upon conquering it was immeasurable.

Beyond the Hillary Step lay the final stretch, leading to the top of the world. The path was a mix of rocky outcrops and snow-covered slopes, and the altitude made each step feel like a monumental effort. Yet, the allure of the summit pushed me forward, and with each stride, I drew closer to my ultimate goal.

When my Sherpa guide Kamdorje looked at me and calmly said, "Just 20 more minutes to the top," a wave of emotions surged within me. Tears welled up in my eyes, catching me by surprise. It wasn't just the physical exhaustion or the thin air that brought me to tears; it was the realization that I had come so far, both in terms of the elevation and the personal journey I had undertaken.

In those few words, Kamdorje had encapsulated the culmination of 10 years of preparation, training, and pushing my limits. The enormity of the moment washed over me, and I couldn't help but shed tears of joy, relief, and sheer disbelief. The summit, which had seemed like an almost mythical destination, was now within my grasp, just a mere 20 minutes away.

The tears were a release, a catharsis of all the struggles and sacrifices that had led me to this point. They were a tribute to the countless hours of training, the determination that had fueled me through difficult days, and the unwavering support of those who had believed in me.

As I continued my ascent towards the summit, the cold air stung my cheeks and the tears that had welled up in my eyes began to freeze. It was an odd sensation – the mix of intense physical exertion and the biting cold causing my tears to turn into icy crystals on my skin. But there was no time to dwell on the cold or the tears, as each labored breath became a precious commodity in the thin, unforgiving atmosphere.

With every inhale, my oxygen mask delivered the vital life-giving air, but with each exhale, moisture from my breath condensed within the mask. It started as a subtle dampness, but as time passed, the moisture accumulated, forming tiny droplets that clung to the mask's interior. Soon enough, the droplets began to freeze, and a layer of frost formed, creating an icy barrier between me and the oxygen I so desperately needed.

The paradox was cruel – the oxygen mask that was meant to sustain me was now hindering me. The more I tried to inhale, the more resistance I encountered. The frozen moisture had sealed the once-open pathways, making each breath a struggle. Panic threatened to take hold as I felt the constriction, the sensation of being unable to draw in enough air. It was a suffocating feeling, both physically and mentally.

In that frozen, oxygen-deprived moment, I knew I had to act. With a gloved hand that felt heavy and clumsy, I carefully reached up to my mask. The touch of my fingers against the frozen surface was like pressing against solid ice. I carefully peeled back the mask, feeling a rush of cold air against my damp skin. It was a risky move, for exposing my face to the elements could lead to frostbite, but the urgency for breathable air outweighed the risk.

Finally, as I crested the summit ridge, the majestic summit pyramid of Everest came into view. The prayer flags that adorned the peak fluttered in the wind, a colorful testament to the triumphs of those who had come before me. With a surge of adrenaline and emotion, I stepped onto the summit, standing atop the world at an awe-inspiring elevation of 29,032 feet.

The panoramic vista from the summit was a breathtaking reward for the challenges endured on the climb. The world below appeared both distant and ethereal, while the mountains that encircled me seemed to bow in reverence to the peak on which I stood. The feeling of accomplishment, of conquering both the physical elements and the doubts within, was overwhelming.

As I gazed out from the summit of Everest, I reflected on the arduous journey that had brought me here. Each camp, each landmark, and each step had been a testament to human resilience and determination. The climb had tested my limits, pushed me beyond what I thought was possible, and revealed the strength that lay within. Standing on the top of the world, I knew that this was not just a personal victory; it was a tribute to the mountains, to the spirit of exploration, and to the unyielding human spirit.

Chapter 15

Reflections

Through eleven journeys to Nepal in the past 10 years, I've etched an intimate bond with this captivating country. Every six months, I find myself drawn back, compelled by a mission close to my heart – orchestrating workshops to foster women's empowerment, nurturing the seeds of leadership and skill-building among these remarkable individuals.

Nepal, with its breathtaking landscapes and vibrant culture, has left me a variety of contrasting emotions. The workshops I meticulously arrange, tailored to ignite women's empowerment, fill me with an indescribable sense of fulfillment. Witnessing the blossoming confidence in their eyes, as they grasp newfound leadership tools, radiates a warmth that reverberates deep within.

Yet, Nepal's embrace is not without its trials. The seismic tremors, the raw power of natural calamities that have reverberated through the land, have left indelible marks – both seen and unseen. The anguish is palpable, shared by those who bear physical scars and those whose emotional wounds run deep. It's a heavy burden to carry, a reminder of the fragility of our existence.

The narratives of friends and acquaintances, once painted with vivacity, now bear the weight of adversity. Some have confronted unfathomable hurdles, their lives forever reshaped by the sting of injury. Others, tragically, have departed, leaving behind an echoing void. Their absence serves as a stark reminder of life's unpredictability.

And then, there are the children – innocent souls deserving of boundless hope and potential. Yet, some still grapple with homelessness, their dreams obscured by the rubble of circumstance. It's a stark reality, a poignant testament to the challenges that persist.

But amidst these shadows, Nepal unveils its resilient spirit. The unwavering determination of its people, an unwavering flame that refuses to be extinguished, stands as a testament to human tenacity. The bonds forged, the sense of camaraderie and shared purpose, have provided an anchor during the stormiest moments.

In these recent years, Nepal has become a landscape of transition for me – a mirror reflecting not only the evolution of the nation but of my own journey as well. Through the peaks and valleys, the victories and defeats, I've grown, evolved, and expanded my horizons in ways I never imagined.

While our pursuit of women's empowerment continues, I'm reminded that growth often sprouts from the soil of adversity. Nepal, with its intricacies and complexities, serves as a canvas where dreams, hopes, and aspirations are painted with vibrant hues. As I navigate the unpredictable path that lies ahead, my dedication to this resolute nation stands unshaken, unwavering in its commitment to a brighter future.

April 25th forever remains etched in my memory, an indelible marker of the earthquakes' anniversary. It was a pivotal moment that reshaped the course of my life. Looking back, I'm relieved to see how far we've come – the shattered homes and schools have been painstakingly rebuilt, and the well-being of the girls is intact. Whenever I return to Nepal, those conversations about the earthquakes still surface, but now they occur in the context of resilience and empowerment. The girls, who have transformed into remarkable and accomplished women, actively engage in CYE workshops, marking the journey from tragedy to triumph.

Workbook to Climb Your Everest

Here is the workbook designed to help you embark on your personal journey to climb your own Everest. I encourage you to take the time to reflect on and answer the questions provided in the following pages. Once you've completed the workbook, please feel free to send your responses to my email. We can then arrange a time to discuss your answers and delve deeper into your thoughts and aspirations. This workbook is a tool for self-discovery and growth, and I look forward to joining you on this meaningful exploration.

1. What's your Everest? What is your impossible, wild goal?

   _____

   _____

   _____

2. Is it connected to a bigger purpose? Why is it important for you to do this?

   _____

   _____

   _____

3. If you float your Everest idea past your best friend/ spouse/ business partner, what do you hear? What does it tell you? Where do you agree with them? Where do you disagree?

_____

_____

_____

4. How would you benefit from not climbing your Everest?

_____

_____

_____

5. How would you benefit from climbing your Everest?

_____

_____

_____

6. Make a list of advantages and disadvantages of climbing your Everest. Having made this list, what insights do you have? What patterns do you notice?

_____

_____

_____

7. After looking at your patterns, which way does the balance tip? Towards continuing to climb or quitting or changing paths?

_____

_____

_____

8. If you have already taken steps towards this goal/Everest what was your misstep? What did you learn from it?

_____

_____

_____

9. What are the actions you are taking or not taking towards your Everest? Big or small actions, write them all.

_____

_____

_____

10. What price would you (or others) pay should you not take on your Everest? (think about your WHY?) (yourself, your family, the world)

_____

_____

_____

11. Who would you be if you fully committed to your Everest?

_____

_____

_____

Your Everest Team

Your Everest team provides essential support, resources, expertise, and motivation to help you overcome challenges, make informed decisions, manage risks, and ultimately reach your goals. They are your partners in this remarkable journey, making your success a collective effort.

Diverse Expertise: A well-rounded team brings a diverse range of skills and expertise to the table. Each member contributes their unique strengths, knowledge, and perspectives, which can lead to innovative solutions and more effective problem-solving.

Shared Responsibilities: With a team, you can delegate tasks and responsibilities based on individual strengths. This allows you to focus on your core competencies while others handle different aspects of your Everest climb, such as logistics, safety, or communication.

Support and Motivation: Climbing Everest is a challenging endeavor, both physically and mentally. Your team provides emotional support, encouragement, and motivation during difficult times. They remind you of your goal and help you stay focused and determined.

Collaborative Decision-Making: When facing tough decisions or unexpected challenges, your team can collaborate to make informed choices. Group discussions allow you to explore various options and consider different viewpoints, leading to better outcomes.

Risk Management: Having a team helps distribute risk. Each member contributes to safety measures, identifies potential hazards, and supports each other during risky situations, reducing the overall risk associated with the climb.

Efficient Resource Management: Your team can help manage resources effectively, whether it's equipment, supplies, or finances. Proper resource allocation ensures that you have what you need when you need it, increasing your chances of success.

Networking and Connections: Team members bring their networks and connections, which can open doors to valuable resources, partnerships, or opportunities that may be beneficial for your climb.

Learning and Growth: Interacting with diverse team members allows for continuous learning and personal growth. You can learn from their experiences, acquire new skills, and broaden your horizons.

Shared Accomplishments: Reaching the summit of Everest is a significant achievement, and sharing it with your team creates a sense of shared accomplishment and camaraderie. These bonds can last a lifetime.

Continuous Improvement: Through regular feedback and evaluation, your team can help identify areas for improvement. Constructive criticism and suggestions for refinement can contribute to ongoing progress toward your goal.

Please answer below questions to get a better perspective about your team.

1. Who do you leave behind? Who doesn't like change? Who is a taker not a giver? Who doesn't see you at you best and view your past versions? Who reminds you of your failures constantly? Who triggers the worst in you?

   _____

   _____

   _____

2. Who is climbing with you? Who has your back? Who is fired by purpose? Who helps you channel your emotions? Who is fierce?

   _____

   _____

   _____

3. Who brings you gentleness? Who offers you encouragement? Who provides sanctuary? Who is unconditional?

   _____

   _____

   _____

4. Who brings you insights? Who create space for reflection? Who helps you open up?

   _____

   _____

   _____

5. Who stretches your ambition? Who is courageous and visionary?

_____

_____

_____

6. Who challenges you? Who is the devil's advocate? Who disrupts the comfortable path? Who causes chaos?

_____

_____

_____

To gauge your team and assess their suitability and effectiveness in helping you reach your Everest goals, consider asking the following questions from your team:

Skills and Expertise:

What specific skills and expertise do you bring to the team?

How do your skills align with the needs of our Everest climb?

Can you share examples of past experiences where your skills were instrumental in achieving a challenging goal?

Commitment and Availability:

How committed are you to supporting this Everest climb?

What is your availability for planning, preparation, and actual climbing?

Are there any potential conflicts or commitments that might affect your availability?

Motivation and Enthusiasm:

What motivates you to be a part of this Everest climb team?

How enthusiastic are you about the challenges and opportunities this journey presents?

How do you envision contributing positively to the team's dynamic and spirit?

Communication and Collaboration:

How comfortable are you with open and transparent communication within the team?

Can you describe a situation where you effectively collaborated with a diverse group to achieve a common goal?

How do you handle disagreements or differing opinions within a team?

Problem-Solving and Adaptability:

How do you approach problem-solving in challenging and uncertain situations?

Can you provide an example of a time when you adapted to unexpected changes and overcame obstacles?

What strengths do you bring to help the team navigate unforeseen challenges during the climb?

Safety and Risk Management:

How familiar are you with safety protocols and risk management in mountain climbing?

What measures would you take to ensure the safety of yourself and fellow team members during the climb?

Are you comfortable following guidelines and instructions to prioritize safety?

Resource Management:

How do you handle the responsible use and management of equipment, supplies, and resources?

Can you give examples of situations where you demonstrated effective resource management?

Team Dynamics and Support:

How do you contribute to fostering a positive and supportive team environment?

Can you describe a time when you provided support or encouragement to a team member facing challenges?

How would you handle conflicts or disagreements within the team?

Adaptability to New Environments:

How well do you adapt to unfamiliar and physically demanding environments?

Are you open to learning new skills and techniques that might be required for the Everest climb?

Long-Term Vision and Contribution:

What is your vision for the team's success and the impact of this climb?

How do you see yourself contributing not only during the climb but also in the overall mission of reaching the summit?

These questions can provide insights into your team members' capabilities, attitudes, and alignment with your Everest goals. Their responses will help you assess how well each member fits into the team and contributes to your collective success. Remember that open and honest communication is key to building a strong and effective team.

Your Mentor, Your Sherpa

Having a mentor as you climb towards your goal, especially a challenging and significant one like climbing Everest, can offer numerous valuable benefits:

Guidance and Wisdom: A mentor provides you with the wisdom and guidance gained from their own experiences. They have walked a similar path and can offer insights into the challenges, decisions, and strategies they employed to overcome obstacles.

Accelerated Learning: Learning from someone who has already achieved what you're aiming for can significantly expedite your learning curve. You can avoid common mistakes, make informed decisions, and adopt effective techniques more quickly.

Motivation and Inspiration: Mentors often serve as a source of inspiration. Their success story can motivate you to persevere through tough times, maintain focus, and stay committed to your goal.

Personal Development: A mentor can help you develop personally and professionally. They may provide constructive feedback, help you enhance your strengths, and work on areas that need improvement.

Network and Connections: Mentors often have a wide network of contacts and connections. They can introduce you to valuable resources, potential collaborators, and opportunities that you might not have access to otherwise.

Confidence Building: Having a mentor who believes in your abilities and supports your journey can boost your self-confidence. Their encouragement and belief in you can help you overcome self-doubt and push your limits.

Accountability: A mentor can hold you accountable for your actions and commitments. Knowing that you have someone to report to can motivate you to stay on track and maintain your discipline.

Problem-Solving: When you encounter challenges or dilemmas, a mentor can offer fresh perspectives and creative solutions based on their experiences. This can help you navigate complex situations more effectively.

Emotional Support: Climbing towards a challenging goal can be emotionally demanding. A mentor can provide empathetic support, lend a listening ear, and offer encouragement during tough times.

Legacy and Knowledge Sharing: Mentoring is often a way for experienced individuals to share their legacy and pass on their knowledge to the next generation. By being mentored, you become part of this legacy of shared wisdom.

In essence, a mentor becomes a valuable companion on your journey, providing you with insights, advice, encouragement, and support that can significantly enhance your chances of success. Whether it's by offering practical guidance or boosting your morale, a mentor can be a crucial asset as you strive to reach your Everest.

Your Walls, what is stopping you from climbing your Everest?

Knowing your walls/fears as you work towards your Everest is crucial for several reasons:

Self-Awareness: Understanding your fears allows you to be more self-aware and in tune with your emotions. This self-awareness helps you recognize when fear is holding you back and allows you to address it proactively.

Identifying Barriers: Fears can act as barriers that prevent you from taking necessary actions or making important decisions. By pinpointing these fears, you can work on strategies to overcome them and remove obstacles on your path.

Preparation: Knowing your fears enables you to prepare mentally and emotionally. You can develop strategies to cope with challenging situations and develop resilience to face adversity head-on.

Risk Assessment: Fears often relate to potential risks or negative outcomes. By understanding your fears, you can assess the actual risks more objectively and make informed decisions based on a balanced perspective.

Decision-Making: Fear can sometimes cloud judgment and lead to irrational decisions. When you're aware of your fears, you can make more rational and logical choices, considering both the potential benefits and risks.

Personal Growth: Confronting and overcoming your fears is a powerful catalyst for personal growth. It pushes you out of your comfort zone and helps you develop new skills, confidence, and resilience.

Goal Adjustment: Knowing your fears allows you to evaluate whether your goals are aligned with your values and passions. It helps you differentiate between fears that are holding you back from pursuing a worthy goal and fears that signal a misalignment.

Empowerment: Acknowledging your fears gives you the opportunity to take control. Instead of being controlled by fear, you can take steps to manage it, allowing you to make progress despite its presence.

Resource Allocation: When you're aware of your fears, you can allocate resources such as time, effort, and support to address those fears effectively. This might involve seeking guidance, acquiring new skills, or building a support network.

Resilience and Adaptability: Knowing your fears enables you to build resilience and adaptability. You can learn to bounce back from setbacks, navigate challenges, and adjust your approach as needed.

Emotional Well-Being: Unaddressed fears can lead to stress, anxiety, and even burnout. By acknowledging and working through your fears, you promote better emotional well-being and mental health.

Ultimately, knowing your fears empowers you to make conscious choices, take calculated risks, and navigate the uncertainties of your journey more effectively. It's an essential part of personal growth and achieving your goals with confidence and determination.

Overcoming fears to achieve your goals is a courageous and transformative process. Here are some steps to help you navigate and conquer your fears:

Acknowledge Your Fears: The first step is to identify and acknowledge your fears. Be honest with yourself about what is holding you back. Write down your fears and thoughts associated with them.

Understand the Root Cause: Explore the origins of your fears. Understanding why you have these fears can provide insights into how to address them. Sometimes, fears are based on past experiences or limiting beliefs that may no longer be relevant.

Challenge Negative Thoughts: Often, our fears are fueled by negative self-talk and irrational beliefs. Challenge these thoughts by questioning their validity and providing evidence to counter them. Replace negative thoughts with positive affirmations and realistic perspectives.

Break It Down: Break your goal into smaller, manageable steps. Focusing on smaller tasks can make the overall goal seem less daunting and help you build confidence along the way.

Visualize Success: Imagine yourself successfully achieving your goal. Visualizing the positive outcome can help reduce fear and anxiety. Create a vivid mental image of yourself overcoming obstacles and reaching your desired outcome.

Seek Support: Share your fears with a trusted friend, mentor, or coach. Having someone to talk to can provide emotional support, encouragement, and valuable insights. They may offer a different perspective that helps alleviate your fears.

Educate Yourself: Often, fear stems from the unknown. Research and gather information about your goal and the steps needed to achieve it. Knowledge can empower you and reduce uncertainty.

Develop Skills: Acquiring new skills related to your goal can boost your confidence and competence. Taking courses, attending workshops, or seeking training can help you feel more prepared and capable.

Take Action: Action is a powerful antidote to fear. Start taking small steps toward your goal, even if they are outside your comfort zone. Each step you take will build your confidence and diminish your fears.

Embrace Failure as Learning: Understand that setbacks and failures are part of the journey. Instead of fearing failure, view it as an opportunity to learn, grow, and improve. Embracing failure as a natural part of the process can reduce its hold on you.

Practice Mindfulness: Mindfulness techniques, such as deep breathing, meditation, and visualization, can help you stay present and manage anxious thoughts. These practices can provide a sense of calm and clarity.

Celebrate Progress: Celebrate your achievements and progress, no matter how small. Recognizing your successes along the way will boost your confidence and motivation.

Remember, overcoming fears takes time and effort. Be patient with yourself and celebrate each step you take toward your goal. By gradually facing and addressing your fears, you'll build the resilience and inner strength needed to achieve your aspirations.

I am always here to support you so please email me your questions and feedback.

Sara@climbyoureverest.org

Made in the USA
Columbia, SC
26 November 2024

47039870R00100